LIKE SHE OWNS THE PLACE

LIKE SHE
OWNS
THE PLACE

Give Yourself the Gift of Confidence
and Ignite Your Inner Magic

CARA ALWILL LEYBA

PORTFOLIO / PENGUIN

Portfolio/Penguin
An imprint of Penguin Random House LLC
375 Hudson Street
New York, New York 10014

Most Portfolio books are available at a discount when purchased in quantity for sales promotions or corporate use. Special editions, which include personalized covers, excerpts, and corporate imprints, can be created when purchased in large quantities. For more information, please call (212) 572-2232 or e-mail specialmarkets@penguinrandomhouse.com. Your local bookstore can also assist with discounted bulk purchases using the Penguin Random House corporate Business-to-Business program. For assistance in locating a participating retailer, e-mail B2B@penguinrandomhouse.com.

LIBRARY OF CONGRESS CATALOGING-IN-PUBLICATION DATA

Names: Leyba, Cara Alwill, author.
Title: Like she owns the place : give yourself the gift of confidence and ignite your inner magic / Cara Alwill Leyba.
Description: New York : Portfolio, 2018.
Identifiers: LCCN 2018014630 | ISBN 9780525533108 (hardback) | ISBN 9780525533115 (epub)
Subjects: LCSH: Success. | Self-esteem. | Motivation (Psychology) | Entrepreneurship. | BISAC: BUSINESS & ECONOMICS / Motivational. | BUSINESS & ECONOMICS / Entrepreneurship.
Classification: LCC BF637.S8 A4639 2018 | DDC 658.4/09082—dc23
LC record available at https://lccn.loc.gov/2018014630

Printed in the United States of America
10 9 8 7 6 5 4 3 2 1

Book design by Kristin del Rosario

While the author has made every effort to provide accurate telephone numbers, internet addresses, and other contact information at the time of publication, neither the publisher nor the author assumes any responsibility for errors or for changes that occur after publication. Further, the publisher does not have any control over and does not assume any responsibility for author or third-party websites or their content.

This one's for you, Mom.
XOXO

You had the power all along, my dear.

—*THE WIZARD OF OZ*

CONTENTS

CONTENTS

INTRODUCTION

am a woman who has spent her entire life obsessively trying to become comfortable in her own skin. I am a woman who has desperately sought ways to embrace every part of herself and to dispel the completely unattainable ideas that society has brainwashed us into believing: that women must be flawless, simultaneously feminine and strong—but not too strong. Successful, but not to the point where that success threatens a man. Beautiful, but not to the point where our beauty intimidates other women. Confident—as long as we don't say it out loud. And skinny. Don't forget skinny.

The world has tried to zip me inside a constricting dress. And after spending years trying to breathe inside it, I'm done. I feel *ready*. Ready for a new way to do life. Ready to challenge the antiquated ideas and pressure from the media that have smothered women for decades. Ready to throw guilt out the window.

Ready to raise my middle finger to diet culture, magazine covers, and self-help books that tell us we're sick and broken. Ready to show women that we are enough, right now, exactly as we are.

I am inviting you to boldly redefine confidence with me. I am inviting you to question everything you were programmed to believe. Because here is one thing I have finally learned: It's not about the thinnest woman in the room with no wrinkles and toned abs and a $4,000 handbag. It's about the woman in the room who knows in her heart that she's a motherfucking boss. It's about the woman in the room who can give herself everything she wants, who makes others feel valued, and who turns that damn room upside down simply by walking into it.

And she's not doing it for anyone's pleasure but her own. She isn't turning heads because she is the most liked, or the most intimidating. She's turning heads because her energy is undeniable. The most confident women are the ones who feel it. And we can't help but see it. And want to soak in every single part of it, because it's just *that* real.

It's time we all realize we can *all* be that woman. It's time we realize that becoming her is as simple as deciding. Can you imagine what your life would be like if you were no longer available for the struggle? If you retired the idea of perfection and decided to fully and wholeheartedly be yourself and—even better—love yourself? Imagine you stopped putting your happiness in the hands of others. Imagine you stopped waiting for validation from external forces. Imagine you became intimate with failure, cellulite, success, wrinkles, imperfection, fuck-ups, and vulnerability. Can you imagine what life would be like if you just decided to *feel good now*?

This is new territory for me, if I'm honest. But it's *fabulous* territory. It's liberating territory. It's empowering territory. And it's work. Maintaining the confidence I've found is a daily practice. It requires patience, dedication, forgiveness, and an incredible amount of self-compassion. It requires taking a good, hard look at my life and knowing when to let things go. It requires asking myself, honestly, what I need. You've probably read that "confidence is a choice," and while that's true, it's more accurate to say that confidence is a series of *repeated* choices to accept yourself.

What does it mean to accept yourself? I used to think accepting myself was a form of giving up. Somewhere along the way, I convinced myself that if I accepted my body, it meant giving up on being healthy. I thought if I accepted my personal best rather than frantically striving for perfection, I would no longer produce quality work. I thought if I owned my flaws, I would somehow let myself go. I did not understand that I could truly love and embrace myself, and be confident, while simultaneously building a better version of myself.

Eventually, through years of hard work, I began to reprogram my mind. I came to understand that the biggest act of self-love *was* bettering myself, being healthy, embracing my failures, and feeling beautiful, but for an entirely new set of reasons. I came to understand that we can—and should—change, but it must all begin with love. I came to understand that an evolving mind is a healthy mind. And we should evolve as a natural part of our growth as women, not because society tells us to or because we're trying to keep up with others.

I've spent most of my life trying to be more beautiful, skinnier, and so on. When I think back on how much time I've spent trying to "fix" myself, it makes me so sad. The time I've wasted starving myself into a pair of jeans or beating myself up over a mistake is time I could have spent laughing, smiling, and loving myself. The time I've spent waiting for the perfect moment is time I could have spent experiencing life. The time I've spent waiting for the right words is time I could have spent wearing my heart on my sleeve and, as a result, feeling all the raw, messy, and beautiful feelings that come with that. It took me a long time to overcome all the bullshit. It took me a long time to develop an unshakable sense of inner peace and become intimate with my intuition. It took me a long time to achieve real, sustainable confidence.

My passion for my own personal development led me to become a certified master life coach so that I could help others too. I saw so many women around me struggling with their self-esteem, constantly questioning their own choices and living for everyone but themselves. I knew I could apply my own experiences and success on my journey to building my confidence, coupled with the training and skills I received from my coaching education, to help women heal. It is now not just my passion, but my life's work. Through my career as a life coach, I have traveled the world, hosted events, written six personal development books prior to this one, and helped thousands of women become empowered and live their best lives.

My goal with this book is to share with you how I have arrived here and how I've helped my clients arrive here, and hopefully save you years of pain, shame, and uncertainty on your adventure to find your own self-worth. Because, girl, I *know* how rocky this road can be. I'm going to show you how to block out all the noise around you and how to free yourself from the opinions and judgments of others. I'm going to teach you how to trust your gut, reclaim your life, and rock what you've got.

I'm going to help you *own the place.*

LIKE SHE OWNS THE PLACE

CHAPTER ONE

Who Do You Think You Are?

I's a chilly spring afternoon and I'm sitting in the chair at my salon getting my roots done. "I think I want pink hair," I blurt out to my stylist, Tarin. It's taken me six months to say this out loud.

She half ignores me, brushing off my monumentally brave admission with a giggle. I've hinted at liking pink hair to her before but never made a declaration as direct as this. As she continues to apply bleach to my head, I explain that I'm serious. "No, really. I'm ready for it," I tell her, clutching my iPhone, which is filled to near capacity with photos of pink-haired strangers and quotes about confidence and living in your truth that I've been secretly collecting for months. My hands are sweating, causing the phone to slip from my fingers and fogging the screen.

I've wanted pink hair for as long as I can remember but was always too fearful to do it. I was terrified of what others would think. In high school in the 1990s, while kids dyed their hair funky colors, I barely found the nerve to use Sun In to give myself a blond streak. I've always felt connected to the "weird kids" or the outsiders—the ones who took chances and dared to live life on their own terms. The ones who risked mockery for the sake of their own self-expression. I admired their audacity, but I struggled with expressing that part of myself, at least from a physical standpoint. I was an insecure teen who struggled with her weight, so the idea of drawing more attention to myself with wild hair seemed completely out of the question. I hated being the chubby girl. And being the chubby girl with weird hair? I just couldn't handle it.

"Seriously? Wanna do it now?" Tarin asks, like a teenager who's just scored a jar of Manic Panic and can't wait to use me as her guinea pig in her parents' basement.

"Should we?"

"Pull up some pictures of what you want. I'll go mix some color and be right back."

The next thing I know, Tarin is rolling a cart toward me with a bowl of cotton-candy-pink dye and a paintbrush. I'm frantically loading my "pinkspiration" photo album on my phone to present to her. I'm excited and scared *shitless*.

A few gut-wrenching, wine-filled hours later, I emerge from the salon with a few baby pink "peekaboo" highlights toward the ends of my platinum blond hair (we decided to ease into things). I meet my cousin for brunch and feel a strange combination of pride and fear. I absolutely love my new hair and I am proud of myself for finally going for it. I am also convinced everyone in the restaurant is judging me.

All of the stories I've played in my mind for so long are now on a loop—*You're thirty-five years old! What the hell are you doing with pink hair? You're too fat for this look, you can't pull this off! You look like a moron.* As I eat my salad, I mentally punch each one of those thoughts out with new, affirming ones. *You look awesome. You've got balls, girl! You finally did it! You are going to inspire someone!* It's taken me a long time, but I've learned that one of the best things we can do when those shitty thoughts creep in is to replace them with ones that feel better. It's not rocket science, but it's definitely science. More on that later.

And honestly? Insecurity creeps in for all of us. Even women who seem like they *own it.* One of my biggest inspirations is Oprah. She is loved and praised by millions of women around the world. To many, she is *the* authority on self-help. Yet Oprah has battled her weight issues publicly for years. She has been open and honest about her struggles with the scale. In fact, in 2009, she appeared on the cover of her own magazine, next to a photo of herself forty pounds lighter with the headline "How Did I Let This Happen Again?" In the article, Oprah admitted that four years prior, when she got down to a slim and trim 160 pounds, she thought she had her weight problems solved once and for all. But after dealing with a thyroid issue and hectic schedule, she hit the 200-pound mark again, and she knew she needed help—again.

The fact that Oprah openly admitted to this challenge and shared what she had been through made us love her even more.

She wrote, "If you're a regular subscriber, you'll notice you've not seen a head-to-toe shot all year. Why? Because I didn't want to be seen." That kind of vulnerability is admirable. She wasn't perfect, and she wasn't pretending to be. She told her story in all its realness—something that takes a hell of a lot of confidence to do. She simply owned it. It's no coincidence her initials, plus her network, spell the word *OWN*!

PATIENCE IS A PART OF THE GAME

Oprah inspires me because she shows us that developing real, sustainable confidence takes time. When I think about my pink hair, for example, those few baby pink highlights that caused me so much anxiety (and excitement) were nothing compared to the bubble-gum-to-the-root bright pink hair I have at the time of writing this book. But in the moment it felt like a massive change. And it was. It was more than a dye job; it was an opportunity to tap into my truth and to explore a part of myself I had buried for so long. I describe that day as my "coming out party"—my new pink hair being my opportunity to practice authenticity on a daily basis and, in turn, develop a sense of confidence I didn't think was possible for me.

The process of leaning into your truth requires patience. It's not an overnight thing, and it shouldn't be. It took me years to arrive at the place where I could start transforming my life and ultimately build my self-worth. Whether it was dyeing my hair pink, leaving a failing relationship, or breaking free from a job that held me back from being my most creative and passionate self, all of those decisions took time. Give yourself the space to evolve, and don't put so much pressure on the timeline. It could take you a week, or a month, or years. And that's okay. As long as you're moving, you're on the right track.

And sometimes moving forward means moving backward, at least temporarily. About a year after I dyed my hair pink, I decided to rent a space in my neighborhood for my business. I had always dreamed of having my own headquarters: a space to write, dream, and host events for women. When the space I wanted finally became available, I made an appointment to meet with the real estate agent and put my name in contention. And I also made an appointment with Tarin. Somewhere along the way, I convinced myself that the agent wouldn't take me seriously if I had pink hair, so back to blond I went.

I remember walking into the salon and assuring Tarin, who was so sad that I was parting ways with my bold color, "I'll be pink again, don't worry, but right now I miss being a blonde." It was a flat-out lie. The truth was, I felt I had to fit inside a box—the one I had so desperately clawed my way out of—in order to get approved to rent that space. See how those limiting beliefs can creep back in at any time? I did get approved for the space, and in retrospect, my hair color had nothing to do with it. I got approved because I was successful, I had great credit, and I was the best candidate. But my initial thought process reminded me that confidence is a journey, littered with twists and turns and old voices that often get their hands on a mic—and sometimes, a bullhorn. I've learned that all we can do is recognize where we feel insecure, choose new thoughts that lift us up, and remind ourselves why we burned that box in the first place.

After getting the rental, I was at my local florist, which happens to also service the funeral home across the street. I buy myself a bouquet of flowers there most Fridays, and as I was picking out my weekly blooms, I overheard the manager taking an order. "I'm sorry for your loss. Who should the 'deepest sympathy' card be from?" I watched him take down the information robotically, then field another call. Emotionless. Dealing with death like it was an order of sesame chicken. Really, I couldn't blame him; it was his norm. It was in that moment that I realized we're all going to die. None of us knows when. None of us knows how. So why are we putting off living? Why are we saving things for tomorrow like it's promised? I caught my reflection in the flower refrigerator and saw my blond hair staring back at me. *That's not me!* I thought. *Where is the pink-haired carefree girl who doesn't care what others think? Where is the girl who broke her own mold?* I took my roses, went outside, and made a hair appointment. A couple of days later, I was back to my (new) roots, and I've never looked back.

AM I AUTHENTIC YET?

It took me a while to grow into my authenticity, and that's okay.

Before we go on, I want to address the term *authenticity* for a moment, because I'm going to use it a lot throughout this book. But what does authenticity really mean? It's a word that gets thrown around often, so I want to clarify what it means and how it relates to confidence, specifically. A common definition of authenticity in psychology is the attempt to live one's life according to the needs of one's inner being, rather than the demands of society or one's early conditioning. In other words, being authentic means *doing you*, girlfriend.

Since that spring day when I began exploring my own authenticity, I've truly been in bloom. My hair has gotten pinker and pinker, and my life has improved as a direct result of that decision. It's been a chain reaction of living colorfully, and over time I have explored my authentic self more and more. Though I've had my minor setbacks, I've been able to be mindful enough to stay true to who I am. I've reignited my passion for creating art, I've taken risks in my business, I've been more vocal in asking for what I want, and I've learned to communicate better in my relationships. And I've dealt with the often-unsolicited opinions of others when it comes to my appearance, which has been a crash course in confidence if I've ever seen one!

And in turn, my self-esteem has soared. In fact, I've coined one of my favorite mantras through this process: Check your fucks at the door. Which ultimately means, do what you want and don't worry about what others have to say about it. Because they will always have something to say, and it's completely out of your control. Remember, one day, someone will be taking down an order for *your* funeral flowers. Sesame chicken death. So let's just do what we want now.

The experience of changing my hair color is an example of building my confidence in a way that felt real to me. It was an opportunity to listen to my gut and carve out my personal path. It wasn't an idea that I got from a magazine, or something listed as a bullet point from an article by an "expert" in the subject of confidence. In fact, I don't believe there are any experts in confidence, not even me. There is no one-size-fits-all approach to this.

How do you know when it's working? The same way you'll know if your heater is working—you'll feel it. Confidence is an incredibly *personal* feeling, and not one that can be defined by a listicle or a series of steps directed by anyone else. You'll quickly notice that while this book is about confidence, I am never going to tell you what to do, or who to be. I'm just going to share my experiences, and the experiences of women I've personally observed, to help empower you to find *your* unique path. The only expert you should listen to? Your intuition.

How do you find your most authentic self?
Listen to your gut.

Aside from observing my own reaction to having pink hair and the way it's made me feel, I've become fascinated by the response from others, and how it's made *them* feel. Something interesting happens when you make a bold choice: You become a mirror for others, showing them what's possible—or impossible— for themselves in their own life, depending on their self-belief. Shortly after I went pink, I spent a long weekend in Chicago. I was stopped so many times by strangers, I actually began counting. I tallied up more than twenty-six people in just four days who all complimented me on my new candy-colored hair. And on the plane ride home, I got to thinking about the reason behind all the attention. I don't think every single one of those TSA agents, strangers on the street, hotel concierges, and restaurant staff necessarily loved my hair color or wanted it for themselves. I think they loved the fact that I had done something daring. I believe they respected my confidence—which had been a direct result of my choice to be authentic—and perhaps they saw it as inspiration to be daring themselves.

Of course, there have been adverse reactions as well. "It's only temporary, right?" was one of the first responses I got from someone who lives in my apartment building. "Cool Halloween hair!" was the compliment I received from a cashier at a local boutique. And my favorite, "Has she gone crazy?" was a comment that made its way back to me from someone who apparently felt triggered by my decision to *think pink*. On a recent trip to London, I observed people staring, whispering, and pointing at me. For all I know, they could have liked my hair, but it sure didn't seem like it. Cultural differences play a massive role in judgment and opinion. So if you're waiting to be yourself until every person on the planet praises you for being you, you'll be waiting forever.

SOCIETY, LIMITING BELIEFS, AND WHY WE DON'T NEED TO "THINK LIKE A MAN"

These mixed reactions are to be expected. We are living in a society that makes it exceedingly difficult to just be ourselves—and to love being ourselves, especially as women. In fact, an eight-year study done by Wiebke Bleidorn, PhD, from the University of California and reported in the *Journal of Personality and Social Psychology*, found that across the board, no matter the culture or country, men had higher self-esteem than women.

And it's really no wonder. While one can argue that women are genetically differently than men, and we possess different sets of traits, we can't ignore the obvious: messages everywhere directed at women, plastered across magazines with advice on how to "get rid of cellulite for good" or "reverse aging" or "think like a man" haunt us. The app store on our phones is filled with line-smoothing, face-blurring technology to help us alter our appearance and filter ourselves into perfection. I don't know about you, but I've definitely fallen into the trap of smoothing out my forehead before posting a selfie on Instagram. It's taken a real effort to explore—and correct—this behavior and to realize that it's completely normal to have lines on my face (what a concept, right?).

On top of the pressure to look perfect, we're expected to embody countless contradictions. On the one hand, bad-ass women are supposed to climb the corporate ladder, crush their competition, and be ruthless in their careers. And yet we're also told to be soft and feminine at home. It's downright over-whelming. In fact, research has found that most men like the idea of dating a smart woman, unless that woman happens to be smarter than they are. Being with a woman who is "too" intelli-gent is intimidating and ultimately a turnoff. To that I say: Find the minority.

A quick Google search on "how to gain confidence" will flood us with the notion that we're essentially screwed when it comes to learning how to feel good about ourselves and build our self-esteem. We are constantly inundated with messages that we're not enough, and that we are broken messes that need fixing. And it's destroying us. We are criticized and made to think that we need to be more masculine or be a "bitch" in order to command respect and develop our self-worth. We're made to believe we need to have a hard, emotionless shell when it comes to feelings and relationships, and an aggressive attitude in the workplace.

And speaking of the workplace, can we talk about that? I've come across many women in my own career who have been bullies. Women who are so defensive that they feel they need to tear others down in order to feel better about themselves. Women who feel they need to be nasty and intimidating if they want to be seen. Through my own work and experiences, I've learned to identify this facade immediately. It makes me sad, because I know we are better than this. And I know where this all comes from.

This toxic messaging that we are not enough begins early in our lives. From the start, we are taught to strive for an unrealistic ideal. According to research, seven in ten girls believe that they are not good enough or don't measure up in some way. An astounding 98 percent of girls feel there is an "immense pressure to look a certain way," especially from external sources. And 74 per cent of girls say they feel pressured to please everyone. This brainwashing begins in childhood and it's not easy to shake off. In fact, it stays with most of us for a long, long time.

In my life coaching practice, I work with women who are fed

up with the struggle and want to make positive changes to become happier. They're sick of living in a hamster wheel of self-loathing and desperately want to feel better but lack the confidence to make it happen. When guiding women on this journey, the first thing we must unpack is *why* they want to change in the first place. I typically ask these women a question I'd like you to ask yourself right now: What do you truly want? And why do you want it? It's so important to clear out all the outside noise and the voices that tell us what we *should* want (liposuction, a sprawling beach house, and a mind like a man), so we can dig deep and figure out what actually excites us on a soul level. We can differentiate healthy change (wanting to pursue our passions, dye our hair pink, or develop a healthier lifestyle, for example) from all the other bullshit that we've been fed. This is the first step to developing sustainable confidence.

If you're reading this book, I sense that you probably want something that, up until this point, you may have lacked the confidence to go out and get. What is it? Feel free to write about it a bit below. This is meant to be an interactive experience, so grab a pen because I'm going to get you thinking.

_____

_____

_____

_____

_____

Once we're clear on what we want, the real work comes in: battling against our limiting beliefs, our desire to fit in, and our fear of judgment. Although my clients are successful, intelligent professionals, and although they have accomplished so much, they still struggle with finding the conviction to live their truths. They still want to please those around them rather than run the risk of ruffling some feathers—or worse, being rejected. They truly want to push past their comfort zones and invite healthy change into their lives, but their fears stop them. They have desires that they are afraid to express, and dreams they've grown accustomed to burying.

I was getting my hair touched up the other day and a woman in her fifties came up to me and said, "I wish I could have hair like yours." I told her she could! "But my kids would think I was crazy!" she replied. "I actually think they'd be pretty impressed with your conviction," I told her. She agreed but didn't feel she could get past the risk of them not accepting her. It was heartbreaking: she was denying something she really wanted to do because she was worried about someone else's opinion.

The question of "What will people think?" comes up more than any other. And I get it! We have been sold lies for our entire lives. As I mentioned, the women I work with are brilliant and talented, but their anxiety often gets the best of them. And it's no coincidence. According to the Anxiety and Depression Association of America, women are twice as likely to have anxiety disorder as men. And the most common disorder to co-occur in women with anxiety is depression. So we're scared *and* sad—not a good place to be. While this statistic is alarming, the great news is it is something we can actively work on. My friend and colleague Dr. Fritz Galette once offered me great advice about anxiety that changed my life. He explained that anxiety is simply an energy, one that we can channel into positivity. One that we can use to propel our ideas. Something that can help us *thrive*. That statement was powerful to me. At the time, I was suffering from my own issues with anxiety, and Dr. Galette's suggestion encouraged me to work on shifting those feelings. I became more mindful of my anxious moments and realized that more often than not, I was basing my reality in irrational thoughts or things that would probably never happen. I began introducing "best-case scenarios" into my thinking and focusing on what could go right. Rather than stuff down those nervous feelings, I addressed them. I worked through them. And I came out stronger.

So when it comes to building confidence, if we can reframe our thinking and view the desire to change as an opportunity to grow and to ultimately *feel* better, we can get ourselves on a positive path. It all boils down to rewiring our thought patterns and writing a new story for ourselves. It comes down to believing that despite our past, and despite our surroundings, we have a *choice* to change. We have a choice to become who we want to be, which for many of us means being a more confident, more self-assured woman.

What choice are you ready to make?

_____

_____

_____

_____

_____

WHAT'S YOUR STORY?

Now that you know what you want, it's important to know where your stories and limiting beliefs about why you haven't been able to get it yet come from. We grow up believing certain things to be true. These beliefs are usually instilled in us during our childhood and usually come from outside sources: our parents, society, other kids, and so on. For me, it went something like this: _I'm the chubby, insecure girl who is kind of awkward and could never dye her hair a wild color._ Somewhere along the way, that's the role I stepped into, and I believed it was who I was. I also believed positive things about myself, like the fact that I was caring, creative, and smart, but the negative voices are often louder than the positive ones, and for me, they were screaming.

My story stuck with me for years, but somewhere in my late twenties, I realized it wasn't serving me. I had to actively undo that programming and start believing different things about myself. And beyond belief—I had to take consistent action to make my new beliefs a reality in order to achieve sustainable confidence. Like actually go and dye my hair pink.

My goal with this book is to lead you on a journey of self-discovery similar to the one I've been on for years. I'm excited to help you discover things you might not have realized about yourself. I'm going to help you figure out how your brain works and, in turn, be able to make sense of the emotions you have probably felt for years (hello, fear and anxiety!) and ultimately master them.

This will take work. Although I believe positivity rules, that does not mean it comes without making a mess first. Rewiring our minds is no easy feat. It takes courage, conviction, and vulnerability. It takes stepping out of our comfort zones and immersing ourselves in experiences that feel different. It takes showing up to our fears, recognizing their presence, and moving forward anyway, even when it feels painful or strange or isolating. For me, it was pink hair. For you, it may look completely different. The most important thing to remember is that getting to know yourself is an intimate challenge, and only you can determine the best path to get there. And if it feels bumpy, I promise you it will be okay in the end. Just hang on tight.

I encourage you to think about who you truly are—without all the baggage attached to the idea of yourself. Without the magazine articles, without the stories from childhood, without the fear of rejection. Who would you be if you were to be your most confident self? Take a moment to answer that in the space below:

_____

_____

_____

_____

_____

And here's something else to think about: If you choose *not* to be that confident person, what do you risk giving up?

_____

_____

_____

_____

_____

Another important cornerstone of confidence to consider: It's not about being like someone else who is confident. It's about being *you*. It's not about emulating the outspoken woman in the conference room with the razor-sharp tongue, or dressing like the self-assured plus-sized model who loves her body. It's about uncorking *your* truest self and owning every part of her. It's about examining every square inch of yourself, keeping what's true, and discarding the rest.

Sure, we can—and should—be inspired by truly confident women who have gotten that way by embracing their true selves. But at the end of the day, it's about inspiration, not imitation.

A woman once told me she was struggling with learning to love her body. She said, "I'm trying to channel Ashley Graham, but it's not working. I'm still beating myself up over eating too much sugar this week and throwing my diet out the window." I explained to her that channeling Ashley Graham would never make her love her body. *Real* confidence comes from loving yourself and all your mistakes and imperfections and still facing the world every day with a loving heart and your head held high. Rather than blaming your insecurity on the external things like blowing your diet, the real work comes from asking yourself what's happening on the inside. Are you happy? Are you prioritizing your overall well-being? Are you doing things that feel good for you?

BEWARE OF THE SUGAR RUSHES

Most of us are used to gaining confidence through what I call *sugar rushes*, like putting on an outfit we feel good in or shedding a few pounds. And sure, those things may make us feel great in the short term, but is that feeling really sustainable? Is that real self-worth that can stay with us for the long haul? I don't believe it is.

My first experience in finding false confidence happened at age eleven. As I mentioned earlier, I was a chubby kid, and not only did it bother me, it was worrying to my mother when she noticed I had gained a considerable amount of weight in a short time after my parents divorced. I was clearly eating to fill an emotional void, and it was a real challenge for me to maintain a healthy weight. I begged my mom to let me join Weight Watchers to help me get a handle on my relationship with food. She obliged, and during the summer of 1991, I lost twenty-three pounds.

I clearly remember walking into sixth grade at my brand-new junior high school that September wearing a size small Gap shirt (a first for me), feeling completely different—not just physically, but emotionally. Suddenly, the cool girls were talking to me. Guys I'd had crushes on for years were finally noticing me. Everyone commented on my weight loss, and everyone told me how great I looked. I was high on all the attention and, at the same time, scared to death that it could go away at any moment. I feared that if I gained the weight back, I'd go back to being invisible.

That experience was the beginning of the disordered eating and unhealthy relationship with my body that affected me for most of my life. I found a quick hit of confidence in my ability to control the scale at a young age, and it was a dangerous game. My anxiety over wanting to keep the weight off caused me to eat more, and before I knew it, I was on a vicious cycle of yo-yo dieting that would bring me anything *but* confidence.

It has taken me twenty-five years to begin to accept and celebrate my body—regardless of my weight. I have now learned that being truly confident in my skin requires much more than finding myself in a certain size jeans. It requires a daily prescription of self-love, forgiveness, and patience. It requires an understanding that sustainable confidence is not dependent on anything outside myself. Rather, it all comes from within.

I used to put my self-esteem in everyone's hands but my own. I felt beautiful only if a man told me I was. I felt successful only if I received a promotion at work. I felt sexy only if I was a certain weight on the scale. I felt validated only if others praised me. I now understand how unhealthy it is to live like that. I now realize that truly owning who you are has nothing to do with other people and everything to do with the love and acceptance you give yourself. I have learned that if you rely on those outside things to deliver your confidence, you will wind up depressed, confused, and on the fast track to self-destruction.

Ironically, being yourself can feel like hard work, especially at first. You'd think being who you are would be the most natural thing to do, right? It's not always the case. As Brené Brown says, authenticity is a daily practice. It's not a quality that some people naturally possess and others don't. It's a choice: something we must work at every single day. In fact, I believe authenticity must be treated like a religion. A dedicated practice, applied to our lives on a daily basis, filled with rituals and affirmations and practical applications. You must wake up every single day and say to yourself: *This is who I am, and this is how I'm choosing to show up in the world.* If we don't claim it, it slips away, and we wind up living inside that tired story and giving up on our dreams. Although it may seem daunting, the reward we experience for committing to authenticity is worth every bit of the work involved. Being yourself and owning who you are is a high like no other.

POWER MANTRA

My authentic self is my natural state. I let go of my fear of being intimately and completely me.

---

n the space below, write a mantra for yourself that inspires you to live authentically.

_____

_____

_____

_____

_____

CHAPTER TWO

What We Talk About When We Talk About Beauty

"You look beautiful!" I find myself saying on a regular basis to women who radiate joy, kindness, and an inner magic that is undeniable. It's less about the way they actually look on the outside and more about the attitude they project about how *they* feel inside. It's an energy.

But this wasn't always how I identified beautiful women. Like most of us, I spent my whole life learning and believing that beauty was a physical attribute. A woman looked beautiful if she had symmetrical features, shiny hair, or a fit, toned body. She was beautiful if she was well put together, wearing gorgeous shoes and a stunning dress. She was beautiful if she was wearing nice makeup that enhanced her features.

I started to redefine the term *beauty* when I noticed people's reactions to *my* beauty around the time I left my job at MTV to pursue my dreams. Suddenly, I was receiving text messages,

Facebook comments, and in-person compliments from people I knew and strangers on the street about how great I looked. "Did you lose weight?" "What foundation are you wearing?" "You look amazing!" I was inundated with these questions and compliments constantly. As great as it felt, it was confusing at first. The truth was, I had not lost weight (in fact, I had gained a few pounds), and I wasn't wearing foundation at all anymore (I stopped wearing most makeup outside of lip gloss and a swipe of eyeliner after I quit my job). So what was it?

Before leaving MTV, I was living in a whirlwind of anxiety on a daily basis. I commuted three hours round trip each day on a bus and train in rush-hour traffic. I worked in the heart of Times Square—or as I affectionately call it, Actual Hell on Earth. I was doing a job that required me to be someone I was not in exchange for a paycheck, which made me feel somewhere between a hooker and a fraud. I desperately wanted to live a life that felt authentic to me: to do what I loved every day, to work from the comfort of my home, to have the freedom to go shopping at eleven A.M. on a random Tuesday, or have a glass of champagne while writing at my desk. I so badly wanted to be able to cook myself delicious, healthy meals and have the energy to work out regularly. Yet, for a very long time, my fear held me back from living that life, and it showed all over my face.

When I finally worked up the courage to quit and take the plunge into being a full-time entrepreneur, my entire world shifted. Suddenly, I was waking up without an alarm clock. I wasn't stuck on a bus all morning packed with other miserable people living inauthentic lives. (Have you ever looked around at people's faces during the rush-hour commute? Yikes.) I was exercising regularly and actually enjoying it. I could take walks and get fresh air in the middle of the day. On top of the lifestyle changes, things inside me changed as well. I felt empowered that I had finally made a choice that was so important to me. I felt fulfilled by a career that allowed me to make an impact in the world. I felt an immense amount of gratitude in every moment. That's the thing about not getting what you want for so long— when you do finally get it, you thank your lucky stars and you thank them all day long. For the first time in a long time, I was in love with life.

So when people started telling me how beautiful I looked when I had changed nothing about myself physically, it only made sense that they were noticing an inner change: a change that began in my soul and was ultimately being reflected in my body. I was happy, peaceful, and slowly gaining confidence— something that had eluded me for such a long time. It wasn't weight loss or a new foundation that was making me beautiful. It was my energy that made me beautiful. What a radical observation.

I encourage you to think about a time in your life where you felt most beautiful. What were you doing? Who were you with? Were you happy? Try to think less about what you looked like and more about how you felt. Sure, a gorgeous pair of designer shoes or a fresh blowout can make us feel great, but what really makes us beautiful is the way we feel about ourselves. Are you proud of yourself? Are you doing things that make you happy? Because let me tell you, if you're hating life and living for everyone but yourself, you will be one unhappy bitch standing in the middle of Drybar in your Chanel loafers. Trust me, I've been there.

AH, A THIGH GAP! I HAVE DISCOVERED HAPPINESS (SAID NO ONE EVER)

It's no secret that we live in a culture that prioritizes looks. We're still having beauty pageants where women are judged by the way they look in a bikini. We still have men's magazines like *Sports Illustrated* that celebrate the accomplishments of male athletes throughout but feature half-naked women on the cover who are celebrated for nothing other than the way they look half-naked. I'll never forget the moment that problem was brought to my attention. I was interviewing Katie Willcox, founder and author of *Healthy Is the New Skinny*, for my podcast. My plan for our chat was to talk about the fact that plus-sized models were now getting more attention from mainstream media. At the time, I thought this was a game-changer, and in many ways, it was. It changed the conversation around beauty ideals.

However, it doesn't change the fact that women are still recognized and celebrated only for the way they look. When Katie and I spoke, Ashley Graham had just landed the cover of *Sports Illustrated* and was the first-ever plus-sized model to do so. There's no doubt Ashley broke a barrier in her industry, but I'd be lying if I said that I truly felt her being on the cover built *my* own personal confidence. Did it help a little? Of course. But just because America's newest sex symbol expanded the definition of beauty doesn't mean our problem is solved. What about the women who still don't make the cut? The majority of women who still feel "less than"? Our arbitrary requirements for physical proportions still exclude most women from the term *beautiful,* and the strongly implied message is that they're less valuable, less womanly. The real victory will be when the size of a woman's lips and the height of her cheekbones and the width of her waist don't determine how worthy of notice she is. Beauty is not found outside us. It's found within.

So how do we drop the idea that Botox and Birkins and "Bikini Bodies" define how attractive we look? And why do we even need to look attractive? Who do we feel is judging us, and why is it even important? Now don't get me wrong. I'm not saying we shouldn't strive to take care of ourselves or carry a luxury purse. Lord knows I love my designer duds just as much as the next woman, and my eyelash extensions rock my world. I'm a girly girl and I love to look good, because looking good ultimately helps me feel good. However, all of those things are simply *accessories* to my own inner radiance. They're not where I start. I spend a hell of a lot more time working on my inside than I do on my outside. And I know that if more women did the same, we'd start a fucking revolution.

Because I have redefined beauty as energy, I am very cognizant about the way I talk to other women about appearances. For example, if I have a good friend who is considering cosmetic surgery and she asks me for my opinion, I am straight up with her. I make sure she knows how beautiful she *already* is. I ask her what's going on in her life. Is she happy? Who are the people she's surrounding herself with? How is she spending her time? If she still insists on going under the knife, I beg her to really think about *why* she's doing it. Is she trying to impress her boyfriend? Is she spending too much time looking at models on Instagram? You'd be surprised at how many women are going to extremes such as painful plastic surgery to feel valued and worthy and to keep up with the women around them.

While we're on the topic of social media, I feel like I need to address what's happening there. I love Instagram and Facebook and all of those platforms when they're used in a healthy way. They have provided me with a space to promote my message of female empowerment and directly connect with my readers. Social media has helped me discover other awesome women who are also sharing positive messages. But it's also created a dangerous epidemic of unrealistic expectations about beauty and women. And although it's no big secret that people are seriously altering their appearance on social media, it doesn't mean we're not affected by it.

In a recent *Refinery29* article, Dr. Carmen Lefevre weighed in on why we still compare ourselves to heavily edited images. "It doesn't really matter if we know a photo is fake or not—we all have an automatic response to things we see, so those kinds of photos still have a psychical impact. Cognitively, we know it's not real, but it still ends up reinforcing an ideal or new standard," she said. "The more time you spend surrounded by certain images, the more you normalize that kind of look." Which is why I've made it a habit to not consume those types of images, and instead look for unedited, unfiltered women who are focusing on their message, as opposed to their image, to be an inspiration and role model.

If you spend hours every day soaking in images of women with prominent collarbones and thigh gaps, they will become your personal standard for beauty. Not only is this unhealthy and toxic, it's also a huge waste of time! How can you use these hours to build yourself up?

On a similar note, have you ever flipped through a women's magazine only to end up feeling depressed and desperate? Nearly every single page is littered with advertisements and articles about what we need to fix about ourselves. Wrinkle creams, flat-belly diets, and ads for fillers and age-defying makeup abound. It's actually incredibly offensive that this is the kind of material that's being shoved down our throats by the media. However, I also know that as women, we feed into it. We are the ones buying the creams, getting the injections, and reading the magazines. There's no doubt that we've been brainwashed into thinking we need to be flawless unicorns who are not permitted to have laugh lines or cellulite, but it's time that we start rejecting the idea that we are not beautiful as we are. We must empower ourselves into believing we are perfect, right now, without all of the enhancements. I am sure every single advertiser would be petrified by a groundbreaking admission like that, and that's precisely why they keep filling the world with their propaganda. Because after all, if we are responsible for redefining and cultivating our own beauty, what will they have left to sell us? Absolutely nothing.

And here is something really important: We have the power, and maybe even the responsibility, as women to change this aspect of the world for the better. If more and more of us stop spending our dollars on toxic products like magazines that only praise women for looking a certain way, there will eventually be fewer and fewer toxic products. Advertisers will say to themselves, "Hmm, it seems like no one cares about looking 'perfect' anymore; let's make something else!" As our preferences change, so will the ideals we consume. Isn't it empowering to realize you can shift demand and make the world better for so many women?

Back to social media—I am much more excited about a woman who is willing to challenge the new status quo and post a photo of herself with zero edits. Isn't that real confidence anyway? In my opinion, editing yourself to look nothing like yourself is a giant red flag of insecurity.

A few months ago, I shared a selfie on Instagram with some beautiful and very raw thoughts in the caption. It was a musing about women learning to stand in their own power. It was meant to empower the woman who read it and fill her up with the courage she may have misplaced, maybe after she gained some weight or lost some hope. It was meant to encourage all of us, myself included, to freely proclaim our places in this world, to erase the lines others draw around our potential.

I decided to post the selfie unedited (other than making the picture black and white). There really wasn't much thought behind not doctoring it. I rarely do anything anymore beyond using a pretty filter here or there because I like the tones and colors and the vibe it can create. I deleted the Facetune app from my phone months ago, not to take some radical feminist stance, but just because I got tired. Tired of smoothing my forehead. Tired of fixing the dark circles under my eyes. And I'm assuming you might be tired too.

I woke up the next morning to a message from a friend who had taken it upon herself to Photoshop my selfie. She sent it back to me with my skin smoothed out, my freckles erased, and my dark circles removed. "Fixed it for you!" the text read.

I felt my stomach drop as if I had just tilted off the edge of a roller coaster. Not because I was hurt or insulted, but because the woman who did this truly did not mean any ill will toward me at all. She is a kind and amazing human, but after looking at my face, unfiltered, she saw a problem. She saw something to fix. And it got me thinking, have we become so used to seeing each other with our lines smoothed over that we have forgotten who we are without masks?

Oddly enough, the more vulnerable I become with my work and my words, the more comfortable I feel sharing a photo of myself with less makeup, or with dark circles, or with a little roll of fat peeking out somewhere. Those are the things that make us human. Those are the things that make us real. And I don't know about you, but I don't want to sweep those things under the rug or blur them out for good.

Some food for thought: How do you feel about removing some of your own filters? How do you feel about letting some parts of yourself show that you may have once altered with the Facetune app and the delete button? Listen. I'm not implying we *must* necessarily give up lipstick, burn our bras, and grow out our armpit hair. I'm not implying we should forgo our personal style or femininity. I'm not saying I'll never use another pretty, moody filter or choose a photo where I think I look best. But there is certainly a line we cross when we alter our faces and our hearts so drastically that the cost of looking good on the outside is feeling pretty bad on the inside. I don't know about you, but my heart is the prettiest feature I have, and it will never, ever need a filter.

How has social media affected your confidence?

_____

_____

_____

_____

_____

I'm sure you're wondering how redefining beauty works when it comes to attraction. It's no secret that most of the time people are drawn to each other based on looks, at least initially. But here's the thing—no matter how classically attractive a woman might be, that attraction isn't sustainable if she's not radiating magnetic, beautiful energy from within. And people notice when a woman's confidence is lacking. While doing research for this book, I asked a handful of guys what it's like to date an insecure woman, and they all responded in the same vein—it's a full-time job. So while a pretty face may land a date, what men want in a long-term, healthy relationship is a woman who feels good about herself.

CONFIDENCE IS CONTAGIOUS

Body image and beauty ideals go hand in hand. I'd like to preface the next few paragraphs by letting you know that I strive to be a very healthy person; I believe we should all focus on our overall wellness. I believe we should move our bodies regularly and lead active lifestyles. I also believe we should eat to nourish ourselves, choosing the best foods we can that support our mental and physical health. I understand that for some people, weight loss is a life-or-death situation, and they are under doctor's orders to slim down to lower their risk for disease and live long, fabulous lives. However, an alarming number of women are a healthy weight but still extremely unhappy with the way they look.

Scientific research suggests we all have a natural weight our bodies are meant to be at. Metabolic suppression is a powerful tool that the brain uses to keep the body within a certain weight range, called the *set point*. The range, which varies from person to person, is determined by genes and life experience. Regardless of how many diets we go on, we'll often gain the weight back because our body has that specific place where it likes to settle. Ever notice you always shift back to the same weight when you come off a restrictive diet or rigorous workout routine? It's not a coincidence.

In neuroscientist Sandra Aamodt's book *Why Diets Make Us*

Fat, she discusses this research and why mindful eating is so much better for us than dieting. She is a proponent of shifting the focus from weight loss to self-care, and her arguments are strong. According to Aamodt, dieting is stressful, and those stress hormones we produce when trying to live on some insane diet plan, like consuming 1,000 calories a day, act on fat cells to increase abdominal fat. She explains that weight anxiety and dieting predict later binge eating and weight gain. Hello? Been there, done that, way too many times.

But regardless, so many women become so obsessed with their bodies and self-image that they are starving themselves and overexercising in order to attain an unrealistic ideal. They are ignoring their set point and not listening to what their body needs. These women are glued to calorie-tracking apps and constantly staring at themselves in the mirror, wishing they had a flatter stomach or thinner arms. I know this because for most of my life, I was one of these women.

When I began to think about beauty, and what it means to me as an empowered woman, I knew I had to give up my obsession with my weight. I knew that if I wanted to walk my walk, I'd have to develop a healthy relationship with my body—the way it is right now. Not ten pounds from now. Not when my legs look more toned. I'd have to challenge myself, and the women around me, to create a "new norm" when it comes to our size. I decided to try to literally change the conversation around weight. Any time I found myself around a woman who was speaking negatively about her body, I'd lovingly offer a new perspective and encourage her to embrace herself. And if I couldn't change the conversation, I'd politely exit it. The people we choose to surround ourselves with are extremely important. If you're around women who focus on their flaws all day long, chances are you'll start to do the same. On the flip side, if you're around confident, empowered women who exude self-love, you will follow suit. Confidence is contagious.

Have you found yourself in those negative body-centric conversations too? Here are some great phrases you can use to inspire the women around you to think differently about their bodies. And, if that doesn't work, advice on how to politely remove yourself from the conversation:

When someone says, "I'm so fat," try responding with, "What do you love about yourself?"

If she can't find something she loves, inspire her by suggesting something you love about her (specifically, something about her mind or something other than a physical attribute).

If she keeps focusing on negative aspects of her appearance, you can say something like, "I'm sorry you feel that way. I think you are beautiful, inside and out. And with all due respect I'd like to talk about something else, because I'm focusing on body-positive conversations now." It can be short and simple. She'll get the message.

I was in London a few weeks ago doing press for my last book, *Girl Code*. I was chatting with one of the local bloggers about the pressures of social media. She was particularly fascinated with the fact that I was "not skinny," in her words, and asked me more than a few times if I found myself comparing my size to other women on Instagram. After I explained my theory on beauty to her, I also noted how harmful it was that we were even having that conversation. "Why are we still stuck on this?" I asked her. And if we're going to talk about competition, I explained, I'd much rather strive to be like the girl who has an inner glow and lights up the room just by walking into it, rather than the girl who is simply thin. A size 2 is just a size 2. Being thin won't make us beautiful. Shooting ourselves up with Botox won't make us beautiful. True beauty is the result of an enormous amount of inner work, self-awareness, and self-love.

It is a very life-altering decision to rebel against the mainstream world that tells us what we should wear, what we should eat, and how we should look. Redefining beauty is a cutting-edge school of thought, and often a very lonely place. I had a conversation recently with a friend who was describing a very famous celebrity as a "goddess." She noted that this woman was so beautiful that she didn't even look human! She didn't agree with this celebrity's life choices or business decisions, but she thought she was gorgeous. I immediately challenged her way of thinking by presenting my own ideas about beauty. "I disagree," I told her. I broke down my new definition of beauty and how this particular celebrity always seemed so angry and unhappy to me. I explained that in my eyes, the negative energy she exuded overshadowed her physical appearance, and I didn't categorize her as a beautiful woman. She couldn't grasp my opinion, and I couldn't grasp hers. Many women will forever see beauty as a physical attribute. They will choose to look at it in a vacuum, ignoring the deeper connection. Not everyone gets it. Not everyone is ready for it. And that's okay. But believe me, recognizing beauty as energy is one hell of a revelation and a *beautiful* place to be.

ADVANCED THINKING

I discovered Ari Seth Cohen's book, and later documentary, *Advanced Style* around the time I was thinking about dyeing my hair pink. I remember poking around on Pinterest to find an image of a seventy-plus-year-old woman with pink hair, because I had written a funny Instagram post about feeling like I needed to be either seventeen or seventy-five years old to do it (*why oh why, Cara?*). A quick search for "old lady with pink hair" led me down a rabbit hole that began to shift my entire mind-set about aging. Fast-forward to a few days later and I had devoured Ari's book, which depicted the most stylish and glamorous older—or "advanced," as he calls them—women in New York City. Along with the glossy photos were inspirational captions from the women, with commentary on everything from embracing old age to feeling confident to why sunglasses are the ultimate accessory. The quotes in the book were empowering. "Some might see it as gray hair, age, genetics, stress, etc. I see it differently. I see it as platinum elegance," Lubi, one of the women featured in the book, said.

The first thing I noticed about *Advanced Style* was that every single woman who was profiled had a zest for her life. They all had their own issues—some had lost husbands, battled cancer, or lost their vision or ability to walk well. However, none of them harped on it. They chose to focus on happiness, and they did not take themselves too seriously. *This* is what makes them beautiful. Can you imagine how your opinion of yourself would change if when you looked in the mirror you focused on gratitude rather than wrinkles?

I've always been fascinated with older women who own their age. My own grandmother, sadly, hid her age from everyone and often lied about it when asked. Unfortunately, she felt that her age defined her as a woman. She did not feel beautiful or valuable as she went into her later years, and it was a major cause of depression for her. Which is heartbreaking—I remember her as being so beautiful, because I remember her for her heart.

My mother's best friend's mother has the complete opposite attitude about aging. Corinne is a vibrant, eighty-five-year-old goddess. She looks like she stepped straight off the streets of Paris, with her fashion-forward outfits and her girlish charm. She is the epitome of glamour, and what makes her even more wonderful is how warm and funny she is. She could have written Emily Post's etiquette book, but she'd never put anyone else down if they used the wrong fork. She knows how to laugh at herself, toss a flower in her hair, and make those around her comfortable. Corinne is truly beautiful, because she believes she is.

When I watched the *Advanced Style* documentary, I was even more captivated by these women who defy the ageism epidemic in our culture. In our society, women are taught to be ashamed of aging and to hide the very natural parts that come along with having the privilege to live a long life. There is nothing wrong with having lines on our face, yet talk to almost any woman and

I can guarantee she has an anti-aging skin care regimen and plans to get "work" done at some point in her future. And we all know what it looks like when women are overfilled and overdone by plastic surgery. I'll never forget a friend saying to me, "I'd rather look like an alien than look old." That is a real problem.

Painful cosmetic procedures to hide aging, such as face lifts, eye lifts, and Botox, have become so commonplace that things like wrinkles or sagging skin—the very normal parts of aging—are starting to look strange. I know women who regularly have "Botox parties" at their homes, where a trained specialist comes in and guests take turns getting shot up with poison while sipping champagne. Yes, Botox is literally poison. Its technical name is *botulinum toxin*—a toxin produced by bacteria first discovered in poorly prepared sausages during the eighteenth century. What happened to good old book clubs or plain old cocktail parties?

I used to take a very carefree attitude about women getting plastic surgery. "Do you!" was always my mantra. However, as an advocate for empowered women, I have to speak up about this. I can't blindly watch women—many of whom I love—go through procedure after procedure in an attempt to postpone the inevitable aspects of growing older, or cut up and fill their bodies with foreign materials because they can't accept themselves. If women did half the work on the inside that they're doing on the outside, they'd realize that all of the time, energy, and money spent on cosmetic surgery is a big fat waste. They'd realize the power in loving yourself, and they'd understand that real confidence comes from embracing imperfection, not nipping and tucking it away.

I read a study that was both sad and alarming to me. A company called A. Vogel (which specializes in herbal supplements to deal with menopause) spoke to two thousand women over age forty-five to gauge their thoughts on aging. To sum up some incredibly depressing stats, more than half of the women felt they'd been judged negatively because of their age. Only 15 percent said they felt confident in any area of their lives. And more than two thirds of the women admitted to feeling ignored by men when they walked into a crowded room. Something needs to change, and it begins with the way we decide to feel about ourselves.

If any of those stats strike a nerve, here are some things you can do right now to turn those feelings of self-doubt into power:

Find a fabulous, "advanced" female mentor. You don't even need to know this woman personally; she can be an actress, a neighbor, or someone you read about in an article or book. Having a positive role model to look up to who owns her age will inspire you and help you combat the scary, negative thoughts about aging.

Challenge yourself intellectually. I started taking Japanese lessons recently as a way to expand my thinking and master a new skill. It's fun, it's daunting, and it's building a hell of a lot of confidence in myself. What have you always thought about doing? Dance lessons? Living in another country for a month? Make a plan and get started.

Create a personal power mantra. A few choice words to remind yourself of your beauty and power will help uplift you during those moments when you start to feel down.

Find a circle of women to connect with regularly. Support is everything! Whether it's a book club, a local meet-up group, or even a virtual sisterhood via Facebook groups, having a trusted "girl gang" to lean on when you want to vent, be inspired, or lend support is key. (Remember: Sometimes helping others is the most empowering thing we can do for ourselves!)

Become a mentor. Speaking of helping others, think about ways you can offer love and guidance to a younger or more inexperienced woman. Look for opportunities in your community, in your industry, or at your office to lend your skills, experience, or even just an ear. It will help you see your own value while motivating someone else to see hers.

I know that the older I get, the wiser I become. I gain my confidence through experience. Through trying new things, and winning and losing. I'm running out of fucks to give about why someone doesn't like me. I'm worrying less and less about what I look like, what someone has to say about my body, or what I can or can't do, say, or wear at my age. And it's addictive. I remember being so anxious about going grocery shopping in my twenties without wearing makeup. I was truly scared of being seen in a less-than-perfect state. These days, I'll proudly show up anywhere without makeup, because I've learned that makeup means nothing compared to who I am as a person.

I understand that some who are reading this who might be older than me (I'm thirty-seven—full disclosure), may think that I just don't understand, because I'm still considered youthful.

However, I've made a confident decision to embrace my age as I age, and to find things to fulfill me outside my looks. I've chosen to place my value as a woman on my spirit, my intelligence, my kindness and compassion for others. And I've chosen to focus on those who are proudly aging, and use them as inspiration for the kind of woman I want to be.

I invite you to think about your own beauty ideals as they are right now. Do you feel beautiful? If so, why? If not, why?

_____

_____

_____

_____

_____

How would your life change if you viewed beauty as energy?

_____

_____

_____

_____

_____

What is one inner change you can make right now to feel more beautiful?

_____

_____

_____

_____

_____

POWER MANTRA

I now choose to view beauty as an energy.
I am no longer available to judge myself or
others based on physical attributes.

CHAPTER THREE

I'm Not Sorry

How many times have you felt guilty for desiring something? Whether it's purchasing a new pair of shoes, leaving an unfulfilling job, or having a glass of wine at two P.M. on a Saturday afternoon, the phrase "I feel guilty" has become the battle cry of insecure women around the world. I am intimate with this mantra because I too was guilty of feeling guilty. All of the fucking time.

About a year ago, I decided to give myself a rare day off. As a busy entrepreneur, I do not do this often. And so I had grand plans. First up was a late-morning bubble bath, where I did not check my emails (major). Then I ordered Chinese takeout for lunch and cued up a *Real Housewives of New York* marathon. I promised myself I'd watch at least two episodes without being glued to my laptop, where I was bound to look at blog comments or moderate my Facebook group. I decided to skip my workout.

I even poured myself a glass of red wine to enjoy my afternoon in pure indulgence—an act that I defended profusely to myself.

My husband had other plans. While I was lounging, he decided to rip apart the closets and organize seven years' worth of Christmas decorations and get rid of old clothes. He assured me that he didn't need any help and encouraged me to relax on the couch and enjoy my afternoon. Yet I couldn't sit still. My guilt weighed on me, and within minutes I was up, trying to help him dig through a mountain of old flannel shirts. "Sit down, babe, enjoy yourself!" he pleaded. And he truly meant it.

"I feel guilty," I told him. And as soon as I said it, I realized those three little words represented a very big problem. Why couldn't I enjoy myself while he worked? After all, we are both adults who chose how we were going to spend our respective afternoons. He was in the mood to organize, because it was going to ultimately make him feel better. So why couldn't I be okay with what was going to make me feel better?

Eventually I left him to the closets while I watched a few good melodramatic catfights with my wine, but the truth is it didn't come naturally to me. I realized after that afternoon that if I wanted to be truly happy—and truly confident in my decisions—I was going to have to become the permission slip I thought I needed. I had to own my choices, every single one of them, and wholeheartedly step into my power. Since then, owning my decisions has become a daily practice for me. And, as a result, it's become easier to do what I want without the attached guilt, because I now understand what I'm trading for that guilt. And it's been one of the best gifts I've given myself.

If you've ever felt the way I felt on my day off, you're not alone. The women I've worked with throughout the years have all been riddled with guilt for so many decisions they've made— even the ones they have yet to make. I can't even begin to tell you how many women feel a sense of haunting guilt for eating French fries, skipping their workout, or wanting to leave a shitty marriage. Guilt, guilt, and more guilt. And where does it leave us? Guilt holds us back from making some of the most life-altering decisions. It strips away our potential for joy. It keeps us stuck, keeps us small, and keeps us very, very unhappy.

In fact, according to a survey by *Stylist* magazine, 96 percent of women feel guilty at least once a day. And nearly half of those women feel it up to four times a day. The women surveyed felt guilty over their eating habits (which topped the list) as well as neglecting their work and their families. Do you think men suffer the same guilt women do? Here's a hint: no.

Dr. Cynthia McVey, head of psychology at Glasgow Caledonian University, said: "Men tend to externalize faults. They fail an exam because 'the room was too hot,' while women are more likely to internalize faults and would be more likely to admit to feeling guilty because 'I am stupid.'" How heartbreaking is that?!

After all the work I've done on myself and all the work I've done with my clients, here's something I've realized: Most of the time, guilt is just the illusion that we've done something wrong. It is an emotion we tap into as a result of our collective limiting beliefs, insecurities, and desire to please those around us. Think about times in your life where you've felt guilty. What brought up that feeling for you? Did you feel guilty because you felt you were letting someone else down? Did you feel guilty because you felt like you "should" be doing something else? Did you feel guilty because someone else might interpret your desires as selfish?

Of course, there are times when guilt is valid. It's natural to feel bad over certain things, especially when you feel you could have done better. For example, you might regret losing your temper in an argument. But we need to understand that as long as we are not intentionally hurting ourselves or someone else, there's no reason to feel bad for our thoughts or actions. As long as we are not out there being reckless with other people's emotions or intentionally trying to hurt someone, guilt is a big fat waste of energy.

Guilt can sometimes lead to self-awareness, which is important as we evolve into the best versions of ourselves. A healthy mind can recognize where improvement is needed and handle things differently the next time around. However, when guilt becomes obsessive and we allow it to rot away our self-worth, we have a problem. When we replay an unfavorable scene over and over again in our minds—for example, an argument we had with our significant other where we lost our cool—it can become unhealthy. This process, called rumination, can spiral out of control, leading us to feel worse and worse as we continually think about what happened.

Have you ever gotten into a fight with your significant other and lost your temper? Maybe you said some things you regret. You probably felt bad afterward, and even though the fight was long over, you continued to think about what you said in the heat of the moment. You may have started feeling guilt and shame over your behavior, and days later, you felt even worse. It's important to realize that we are imperfect human beings, and we all make mistakes. It's okay to take some time to reflect, and to apologize if you feel you were out of line, but you've got to move past it. You've got to stop ruminating and move forward with self-compassion. Where will continuing to feel guilty take you? Most likely, it will ruin your mood, impact your health, and cause you major stress. If you catch yourself ruminating or obsessing over guilt, one of the best ways to move on is to do something for yourself that makes you feel powerful and calibrated in that moment. Work out, read a book, or go shopping. Doing something that makes you feel rested, creative, and productive will help you redirect your thoughts to something more positive.

When asking my clients what brings on guilt for them, I've heard it all: They've felt guilt for wanting to exit a toxic relationship, guilt for being more successful than their partner, guilt for working too much and not being there for their children, guilt for not working enough, guilt for not being a "good enough" wife, guilt for wanting a raise at work, you name it. And while all of these scenarios may look different on the outside, it all comes down to one thing: our conditioning. We were all raised with specific beliefs. We've carried those beliefs with us throughout life, and for better or for worse, they've shaped us. And until we work hard at challenging them and really digging into the root of whether they are true for us now, we'll continue to live with these feelings.

I invite you to think about an area of your life where you feel guilt:

_____

_____

_____

_____

When and where did you learn to feel guilty for this?

_____

_____

_____

_____

How would your life change if you released that guilt?

_____

_____

_____

_____

_____

Guilt isn't always something we bring on ourselves, either. We all have those friends or family members who know just what buttons to push to manipulate us into feeling like crap. If you've ever been the victim of a guilt trip, it's important to understand that the person trying to make you feel guilty is exhibiting a form of manipulation and control—no matter how innocent it may seem. This is an unhealthy behavior, and it needs to be recognized as such.

Here are some common examples of guilt trips:

"I need you to help me with my résumé tonight. I know you have dinner plans, but if I don't get this job, I'll be crushed. And you're so good at this kind of thing!"

"If you don't come with me to this party, I'll just die. My ex is going to be there and I will have a panic attack. If you're a good friend, you'll cancel your plans and come with me."

"Please let me stay at your apartment. I can't afford a hotel right now, plus we'll have so much fun!"

Guilt trippers will disrespect your boundaries, attempt to push past your "no," and always put themselves first. So what's a woman trying to build her confidence and assert herself to do? Here are a few ways you can stand your ground and draw a line in the sand for these master manipulators.

Recognize the guilt. You probably know you're being guilt-tripped, so make the guilt tripper aware of that.

Let them know how it makes you feel. Be honest. Let them know that by trying to guilt you into agreeing to something, they will only wind up pushing you away, and possibly making you feel resentful toward them.

Request that they drop the guilt and be direct. Just as you're trying to be more assertive, encourage the guilt tripper to do the same. Empowered women don't need guilt or mind games to communicate effectively.

Stand your ground. Let them know that you have created a new boundary and you refuse to be treated this way anymore.

Feeling guilty is a direct result of people pleasing. As women, many of us were raised to want to be liked, to please others, and to be "good." For many of us, society, culture, and religion play a major role in the way we behave. We are taught to live by a certain set of values, and putting ourselves first is typically at the bottom of that list. Because of these ideals, we must be careful— there is a fine line between having morals and respecting others, and living to make others happy. I invite you to examine that line in your own life and ask yourself if it is possible to strike a balance. How can you maintain your values but still make yourself and your own happiness a priority? How would your life change if you dropped the guilt around prioritizing yourself? This, I believe, is one of the main components of developing sustainable confidence. For some, it can be one of the most challenging steps to take, but when you finally take it, you will experience a sense of freedom like no other.

NAVIGATING MOM GUILT

I once had a client (we'll call her Valerie) who was an incredibly passionate blogger, and also a mom. One of her favorite things to do was set aside time for herself to write. After dropping her kids off at school in the morning, she'd come home, put on music, light the candles, and get to work. Those few hours to herself helped her develop her voice, express herself creatively, and ultimately build her confidence. It was her "me time" and she looked forward to it every day. But when summer rolled around and her kids finished school for the year, her time to write would be cut in half—if not gone completely. Valerie told me she felt guilty for not spending more time with her kids when they were home, so she gave up her writing for hanging out with them by the pool and watching movies. For the first week or two, she loved it. She was having a ball with her kids, and they loved having time with their mom. But by week three, she started to feel like something was missing. She was behind on her blog, and she hadn't had a chance to feel creative. Even though she longed for that time to focus on her blog, she felt guilty for wanting to take time for herself while her kids were at home.

Each week on our calls, Valerie would tell me how lost she felt. She had given up a large part of her own identity by trading in her writing time for spending 100 percent of her time with her kids. When I asked her what her ideal situation would be, she told me that she'd love to be able to carve out "writing blocks" throughout the day while her children played outside. When I asked what was stopping her from doing that, her reason was, you guessed it, guilt.

Eventually, through a lot of reprogramming, reframing, and honest discussion, she came to understand that if she wasn't focusing on her passion and creativity—the parts of her that made her feel complete—she wasn't going to be the best mom she could possibly be to her kids. She had spent so much time building her confidence by being her truest self, and we had to make sure she didn't lose that. We examined where her guilt was rooted, and as it turns out, her mother was absent during her childhood. She would pop in and out of her life, and when she was present, it wasn't good. At a very young age, Valerie vowed to never be like her mother, so she overcompensated when she had her own kids. Although it's important to be aware of who you *don't* want to be, you can't let those feelings become so strong that they strip away your own identity. We got Val to a place where she could finally let go of those deep-rooted feelings of guilt, and everything changed. She started to write more and more, and she felt happier, more centered, and more energized. She got herself back, and her kids got the best version of their mom.

Another thing I had Valerie consider (and I'll ask you the same thing if you're also a mom): What kind of example do you want to set for your children? Do you want them to see you exhausted, drained, and bending over backward for everyone else? Or do you want them to see you as powerful, fulfilled, and happy? We've got to set a new example for the next generation of women and finally break this damn cycle of guilt.

A dear friend of mine named Tara had children a few years ago, and because of her own guilt, she felt she should quit her job and be home with her family full time. She essentially gave up her own dreams and career goals to be there for her children. At the time, she felt this was the best choice because she would have felt guilty for putting them in daycare. But after a few short weeks, Tara began to miss the parts of herself beyond motherhood. She'd thrived on having a career, on getting out of the house every day and using her talents. Despite those aching feelings of unhappiness, she stayed home for years, and one day when her daughter was in first grade, she came home from school and handed Tara a piece of paper. "Today our teacher asked us what we want to be when we grow up!" her daughter said. Tara asked her what her answer was, and her daughter proudly told her, "I said, 'Nothing! I don't want to have a job. I want to be like my mom.'" Tara's heart sank, not because she wasn't proud of being a mother (which is far beyond a full-time job), but because her daughter echoed her feelings of being unfulfilled. She wanted to raise her daughter to have passion and dreams, because that was what she had sacrificed in her own life. She gave up all of those things thinking she'd give her children a better life, but in reality, her daughter was planning to follow right along in Tara's footsteps. It was as if she saw those limiting beliefs being planted in her daughter, right in front of her eyes. Needless to say, Tara immediately went back to school, finished her degree, and has now achieved her goal of becoming a full-time teacher. Both she and her daughter are very proud.

I want to stress that there is absolutely nothing wrong with choosing to stay home with your children if that's what you want. There is also nothing wrong with going out and working full time if that's what you want. And there's nothing wrong with having no kids at all. Developing sustainable confidence is about owning your choices, dropping the guilt about what others will think, and not being afraid to bust out of the boxes we stuff ourselves into. Most importantly, we must realize that guilt is a feeling we choose. We can choose a new feeling, like being empowered, just as easily.

Guilt is *just* a feeling. You have the power to change how you feel, for the better!

Here's a visual that helps snap me out of my own feelings of guilt. I ask myself, when I'm a pink-haired eighty-year-old woman telling stories with my girlfriends, will any of it matter? Will I say to myself, "Thank God you got up and organized that closet with your husband! You wouldn't want him to think any less of you for actually taking a day off!" It's absurd to spend so much time feeling guilty about things that won't really make a difference in the long run. Live your life. Make yourself happy. And leave the damn guilt at the door. And if you're worried about what others think of you, remember—the people who truly care about you want to see you at your best. They don't want a burned-out, overextended version of you. They want to see you vibrant, connected to yourself, and alive.

SOULCYCLE, GUILT CYCLE, AND LEARNING TO RIDE OUT CHANGE

I never loved working out. In fact, I despised it. Until I discovered SoulCycle, an indoor cycling workout choreographed to the beat of (extremely loud) rock music. For two solid years, I was a devout SoulCycler. I rode religiously anywhere between three and five times a week. I was obsessed. I created my work schedule around my SoulCycle classes. I thought about my rides nonstop. For the first time ever, I saw my body changing and becoming stronger. I felt more clearheaded, less anxious, and more creative. It honestly felt like being in love. But around year two, I started to feel my mind and my body burning out. What had once felt new and fresh and challenging began to feel routine. In retrospect, I realize this was completely normal, but I struggled with realizing it at the time. My workouts began feeling like a chore rather than that exhilarating rush they once were, and I felt horrible over it. My honeymoon period was over.

I began canceling my classes more frequently and taking a few days off at a time (something I had never done before). Soon

I was taking weeks off. Although I clearly needed the break, the overwhelming sense of guilt I felt was unbearable. I didn't want my relationship with SoulCycle to change, but it was happening in front of my eyes. All of the scary thoughts floated around in my mind: I was going to lose all the hard work I had put in (conditioning yourself for those rides is no joke), my body was going to get soft again, my anxiety would come back, and I'd suddenly begin to fail in my business. I was allowing myself to ruminate in my guilt big-time. I knew something had to change, and it had to begin with the way I viewed my time away from SoulCycle. Rather than look at myself as a failure, I saw my time off the bike as an opportunity to recharge my body and spirit. I imagined how great I'd feel after taking that hiatus and how fun and fresh my classes would be after being away from them for a little while. I chose self-compassion over guilt, and it changed everything. I eventually started riding more regularly again but promised not to hold myself to an unfair standard. I was going to ride for fun—exactly the reason I had begun. I was going to ride without judgment. And if I skipped a class, I was not going to beat myself up for it. Guilt was not serving me. So it had to go.

The things that make us happy and fulfilled will always be in flux. If the exact same thing is making you happy forever, maybe that's a bit unhealthy—or at least worth exploring. Are you happy, or are you comfortable? We're meant to evolve, and we're meant to fall in love with new and exciting challenges. If something is no longer working for you, the way SoulCycle was not working for me at the time, release the guilt around it. Focus that energy into taking a break from it, or perhaps finding your next chapter. Choose to live in a state of flow rather than resistance. It's a hell of a better ride.

I've found it helpful to create affirmations to help reprogram the way I think. A powerful affirmation in dropping guilt is as follows:

I will no longer be the woman who defends her thoughts, opinions, or actions to herself or anyone else.

Repeat that with your morning coffee, before bed, or any other time you catch yourself feeling bad for being, well, yourself.

In the space below, create your own affirmation for letting go of guilt:

_____

_____

_____

_____

SHITTY UBER DRIVES AND FLAT CHAMPAGNE: HOW TO SET BOUNDARIES

Aside from "I feel guilty," there is one other harmful phrase that is keeping confidence at bay for so many women. That phrase is "I'm sorry." This phrase perverts even the smallest parts of our daily lives. How many times have you replaced the words "Excuse me," "What?" or even "Hello" with "Sorry"? Guilt seems to live in our subconscious, and we even express it when we don't necessarily mean it, because we feel like we're supposed to feel it! Do you ever feel like a "sorry" robot?

I will never forget one of the first times I bit back the apology I was about to make and chose confidence over self-doubt. Man, did it feel *good*. It was ninety-seven degrees and I had just finished working out. Dripping with sweat and navigating an intensely humid New York City afternoon, I decided to stop in the supermarket to grab a few things before heading home. Six heavy bags later, I knew the only way to make it home in one sane piece was to get an Uber. As the driver approached my building, he slowed down, and rather than make the U-turn (or go around the block) to leave me in front of my door, he attempted to leave me across the street, in the middle of traffic. I sat in the backseat, assuming he was waiting for traffic to pass so he could make the U-turn. He didn't. I thought: *Hmm, I don't want to annoy this guy, but I* really *don't want to carry these damn bags.* He looked at me in the rearview mirror, unlocked the doors, and waited for me to get out of his car. Then, like vomit, "Sorry" dropped into the back of my throat. For what seemed like the first time ever, I forced myself to swallow it. I asked him to turn around and leave me in front of my house. "Oh, you want me to turn around?" he asked, sounding confused—and annoyed. "Yes. Yes I do," I said. He made a U-turn. I got out of the car and went on with my day, without apologizing.

This little story is about so much more than an Uber ride for me. A few years ago, I would have let that driver leave me in the middle of the road, and I wouldn't have said a peep, other than "I'm sorry!" after he got irritated. It would have bothered me for days that I'd paid for an Uber and hadn't gotten my money's worth—because I hadn't had the confidence to get my money's worth. A few years ago, I was terrified to ask for help at work when I was drowning in projects, so I suffered in silence and worked myself into complete and total exhaustion. A few years ago, I was too afraid to tell a boyfriend that his behavior was disrespectful and abusive, so I remained in a toxic relationship for way too long. A few years ago, I was way too insecure and way too worried about what other people thought of me to dare ask for what I wanted—even for the things that involved a base level of respect.

This got me thinking about the way so many of us live. The behavior we accept from others is a direct reflection of how we feel about ourselves. It's not just about asking an Uber driver to leave you at your door, or slow down when he's speeding, or put the air conditioning on if you're hot (all things I have confidently asked for when needed—after years of self-coaching). It's also about asking for a raise at work when you damn well deserve it. Or saying no to a man who is making inappropriate sexual advances toward you. Or cutting off an unhealthy friendship with someone who treats you poorly. Or speaking up when your champagne comes out and it's flat. (Do you know how many servers I've apologized to because they served me a bad drink?) You get the idea.

So why are so many of us still obsessed with saying "I'm

sorry"? Some research suggests that women are so worried about coming off as rude that we apologize when we really should be direct. According to a study in the journal *Psychological Science*, women have a much lower threshold for what constitutes offensive behavior. In turn, this causes us to apologize more—even when we should be assertive. It causes us to use "I'm sorry" as a buffer to smooth things over when, in many cases, it's actually the other person who should be saying it.

Can you relate? I'm sure you can count more than a handful of times where you've started a sentence with "I'm sorry, but . . ." or found yourself apologizing when you did absolutely nothing wrong. Have you ever sent cold food back in a restaurant, only to apologize to the server for it? I know I have. May I remind you that you or I did not cook that food, and that we should be receiving food the way it's meant to be served? Have you ever rung your neighbor's bell because they were blasting their television late at night? I bet you stood at their doorstep and began with, "I'm sorry, but can you lower your TV?" What about emailing a coworker and following up on a request? I'll bet you apologized for that too, even though it was the coworker who was late on delivery.

I think we overuse apologies because we are hardwired to be kind, nurturing creatures. We don't want to piss people off. And even scarier to us, we don't want to be disliked. But you must understand that asking for what you want or need does not make you a bitch. Being assertive does not make you difficult to deal with. Having high standards does not make you a "princess" or "high maintenance" or any of these other bullshit terms the world likes to put on women who are confident.

Think about the women you admire most. Are they the kind of women who hang their head down and apologize for everything? Or are they the women who know their worth and confidently assert themselves? I live for women who are direct and firm but do it with the utmost respect for themselves and those around them. I think it's important to note that you can live a guilt-free, unapologetic lifestyle and still be kind and loving. The two are not mutually exclusive.

You should never apologize for chasing the things you love.

Here are a few scenarios where you can use a new phrase rather than "I'm sorry":

If you accidentally bump into someone. Rather than say "I'm sorry," say "Pardon me."

When responding late to an email. Rather than say "I'm sorry for taking so long," say "Thanks for your patience while I took a few days to respond."

When you're following up with someone. Rather than say "I'm sorry for following up," simply say, "I'm following up."

When you're expressing how you feel. Rather than say "I'm sorry, but this is how I feel," drop the sorry and simply say, "I feel . . ."

It's time to create a new list of values for yourself, so that next time the S-word tries to slip its way out, you can swallow that shit. In the space below, answer the following questions:

What's important to you?

_____

_____

_____

_____

_____

What do you deserve?

_____

_____

_____

_____

How do you want to feel every day?

_____

_____

_____

_____

_____

What are you done apologizing for?

_____

_____

_____

_____

_____

G et crystal clear on what you value. Once you define who you are and what you stand for, it's easier to release the feelings of guilt about things that do not align with how you want to feel. Once you know what you deserve, and really believe it, you'll stop apologizing for things that aren't your problem.

POWER MANTRA

I am my own permission slip.
I release guilt because it no longer serves me.

CHAPTER FOUR

Vulnerability Is a Superpower

I had no idea that being your authentic self
could make me as rich as I've become.
If I had, I'd have done it a lot earlier.

—OPRAH

A few Decembers ago, I had the opportunity to see Stevie Nicks in concert while in Chicago for business. I've been a huge fan of hers since I was a little girl, so you can imagine my excitement when I learned she was playing a show on my one free night in town. When I think of Stevie Nicks, a few things come to mind: a sexy, raspy voice; black capes; and magic (in that order). She is a fixture of rock and roll, having reinvented herself more times than I can count—from a young, demure, gypsy-like bohemian in the seventies to a spellbinding man-eater twirling through the eighties to the cape-cloaked Goddess of Rock that she is today. At seventy years old, this witchy woman still tours, records, and commands sold-out arenas around the world. And that icy winter evening, I was about to experience her magic firsthand.

Pumped full of cheap concert wine, I squeezed my husband's

arm as Stevie took the stage. She plunged right into her first song. Swaying along with the droves of other bewitched women in the crowd, I chanted the lyrics to "Stop Draggin' My Heart Around." I hung on her every word as she paused to reflect on the inspiration behind each song before performing it. But then, in a moment, the energy shifted.

Stevie looked directly at the audience and admitted that she was not only thrilled to be with us—she was downright petrified. As she stroked the black and silver ribbons that dangled from her microphone, she told us, "I am so nervous, you guys! I was nervous in New York the other night, and I'm still really nervous. I hope I do a good job for you." The crowd roared, and in that moment, it seemed like Stevie could do no wrong.

I swiftly made a mental note: *Remember this.* Having been to hundreds of rock shows, I have never once heard an artist openly admit to the crowd that they were scared shitless to be up on that stage—especially someone as seasoned, successful, and phenomenally talented as Stevie Nicks. And I had never imagined that an admission like that could make the crowd swoon. This was getting interesting.

I began paying close attention to Stevie's stage banter. At one point, she forgot her piano player's name while giving a heartfelt introduction to him. "I can't believe his name just slipped my mind. I must be having a senior moment!" she laughed. The crowd laughed with her, and I watched as she took what could have been an embarrassingly disastrous situation and made light of it, simply by being herself.

Despite her anxiety, Stevie commanded the stage and put on

the best show I have ever seen. It was in that moment that I realized *real* confidence comes from the ability to expose yourself, flaws and all, and still follow through with your self-expression. Real confidence is about being able to see yourself as imperfect and love yourself for it. I think many of us feel that confidence comes *after* we achieve perfection—which never happens because perfection doesn't exist. We wait, sometimes an entire lifetime, for confidence to come, as if it's some magical feeling that is available only to those who have passed test after test and finally, somehow, stopped failing.

As a woman who has struggled with deep insecurities, I've spent much of my life fascinated with women like Stevie, who seem to ooze confidence and have an effortless yet electrifying energy about them. I've studied these women, read all the *Cosmo* articles about them, and tried to "fake it till I make it," but I was never able to achieve a long-term, sustainable sense of self-esteem. Sure, I got a quick high from losing ten pounds; buying the latest, hottest designer purse; or getting a promotion at work; but those fleeting moments did not last, and I found myself back at square one, constantly searching outside myself for validation and the keys to my own self-worth. That lack of confidence often stifled my ability to challenge my fears and ultimately live better.

Stevie's rawness inspired me that night in Chicago. A woman whom I had always admired for being so strong and self-assured was suddenly touchable. Watching her in action really lit a fire in me to begin unpacking what true confidence looks like. Her ability to be so vulnerable—and own it—woke something up inside me. That night, I realized that vulnerability was a superpower, and that the keys to unlocking my own self-worth were not inside a Chanel bag or a pair of size 8 jeans—they were within me all along.

It wasn't too long after the concert that I needed to sprinkle some of Stevie's magic dust on myself.

In September 2015, I found myself on a flight to Tokyo, reading and rereading a PowerPoint presentation I was about to deliver at the American Chamber of Commerce in Japan. I had meticulously put together a detailed presentation about the power of personal branding, and I had been enlisted to deliver it to fifty of the ACCJ's international members a few days later. As I nursed my third glass of red wine about eight hours into that exhausting flight, I desperately tried to memorize statistics and case studies about fictional women I had given names like Yuki and Rita. As someone who loathes PowerPoint presentations (I don't even use note cards, let alone slides), I saw this as a foreign experience in more ways than one. I never went into a meeting without a planned speech, even during my corporate career at MTV, but I prided myself on being able to command a room in a conversational and authentic way. Every part of this ACCJ talk felt completely *inauthentic* to me, but I trusted the advice of those who had lived and worked in Japan and convinced myself that PowerPoint was the way to go in this situation.

Authenticity: the attempt to live one's life according to the needs of one's inner being rather than the demands of society or one's early conditioning.

That following Thursday, my taxi pulled up to the Place of Tokyo, a breathtaking banquet hall with stunning views of the Tokyo Tower. I hopped out, ready to take on my presentation. With a few more hours of review under my belt, and a glass of (sparkling) liquid courage to prime me, I felt ready. Though I still wasn't quite sold on the idea of the slides, I felt relatively confident about my ability to deliver a clear and inspirational talk to the audience. The members slowly rolled in, taking their seats in the sun-soaked room to enjoy an elegant lunch before my presentation. I chatted with the president of the organization while eating sashimi and sipping green tea. Just as dessert was to be brought out, I was called to the stage.

"It's my pleasure to introduce author and master life coach Cara Alwill Leyba!" The chairwoman gave me a stunning introduction, soothing me momentarily, and before I knew it, I was up. With my laptop still closed, I spoke to the group naturally and gracefully, thanking them for having me and talking candidly about my first trip to Tokyo the year prior— the trip that ultimately inspired me to quit my full-time job at MTV and pursue my dreams. The crowd was engaged, and a few moments later I was finally ready to start the show.

I can do this, I thought, as I opened my laptop and cued up the first slide. I read the title proudly: "The Power of You: Why Everyone Can Benefit from Building a Personal Brand through Social Media." I clicked through to the second slide, which included a short bio of myself. I read it aloud. This immediately threw me off, since I had just spent a good seven minutes introducing myself and sharing my background. *Did that sound stupid?* I thought. *Skip it. Move on to the next.*

I clicked through and read the next slide to myself. "I'm passionate about social media, and I'm excited to share that with you today!" I paused as I read the sentence again. *Was I supposed to say that out loud?* I stared blankly at the screen and then quickly blurted out the quote. I felt my face begin to burn. I sped through the next few slides, fumbling over my words more and more. By slide six, I had completely lost my shit.

I realized I'd read the exact same sentence four times. It was when I saw a German woman in a power suit racing toward me from the back of the room with a glass of ice water that I knew it was over. I was experiencing a full-blown panic attack during my first international speaking engagement. I had gotten in my head so much that I couldn't regain control. I felt light-headed, hot, and disoriented. My worst nightmare was coming true.

I had two choices: run out of the room as fast as possible, or buck up and own it. I sipped my water and took a few deep breaths. "Can I be real for a sec?" I asked the attendees. "This is not easy!" Everyone laughed. I felt the weight of the room lift immediately. Up to that point, most people were watching me in horror. I can remember the look on my brother's face specifically. It was half smile, half panic: the kind of look someone gives you when they have to tell you that your gorgeous, exotic outdoor wedding isn't going to happen because there's a monsoon coming. You know, *that look.*

I realized my only reprieve here was to find a way to break the ice. I thanked the crowd for being so patient with me and admitted my obvious nervousness. "I really thought I had this public speaking thing down. Must be the jet lag and all those Sapporos over the past few days!" The audience giggled. A sense of calm washed over me as I looked out onto all the smiling faces that seemed relieved that I was owning my little shit show. Despite the train wreck that had just occurred, I knew I had one secret weapon: the ability to make people feel comfortable. I continued on with "The Power of You," and with a few more jokes dotted throughout to lighten the energy, I successfully made it through the rest of my presentation. I even think I got a few solid points across.

It was time for the postlunch reception, and before I could make a beeline for the nearest exit, a woman came up to me. "I've just got to tell you, that was the best presentation I have seen all year. You were just so real. It was so refreshing." I stood there in disbelief, assuming she felt bad for me and was trying to make me feel better. We chatted for a few moments, and just as I was about to grab my things and race out the door to avoid any further embarrassment, I suddenly noticed a line of people waiting to speak to me. Person after person commended me for my authenticity and ability to be vulnerable. "I couldn't have recovered the way you did. You just owned it," one man told me. "That was the best presentation I've ever seen. You were so authentic," another woman said. I was shocked by the overwhelmingly positive response.

In retrospect, looking back to that experience in Tokyo, I feel extremely fortunate. I know that day shaped me in a massive way. It equipped me with the tools I needed to power through any less-than-ideal circumstance in life or in business. It gave me a powerful story to share with my clients, and with you. It made me realize how important it is to be relatable. And it reminded me that I have everything I need within myself, as long as I am willing to be vulnerable. Just like Stevie. Just like all of the other incredibly brave women who are out being unapologetic. Forgetting names, forgetting their lines, and sometimes even forgetting themselves.

PERFECTION IS BULLSHIT

Many of us grew up with the idea that perfection is the pinnacle of success. We were programed to believe that progress is just that: progress. Nothing to learn from, and certainly nothing to celebrate. But what if we reframed our thinking to believe that progress is actually more valuable than perfection? What if we believed that we could unlock some of life's greatest lessons within those messy moments, like my day in Tokyo? What if we believed that our ability to be soft, raw, and real could ultimately set us up for our greatest success? UFC fighter Ronda Rousey said it best: "Here's the thing about being perfect: perfect never gets truly tested, perfect never gets to silence its critics, perfect never gets a shot at redemption."

Allowing yourself to be vulnerable and share your truths, no matter how imperfect they may seem, is important. This does not mean you shouldn't strive to be your best self. This does not mean you should throw out your standards and accept half-baked efforts from yourself. What it does mean is that the sooner you can become okay with flubbing your lines onstage, forgetting someone's name, or falling flat on your face—physically or metaphorically—the sooner you can liberate yourself from self-loathing, self-doubt, and insecurity.

I encourage you to think about a time when you felt exposed. A time when you may have made a mistake, said something you wished you could take back, or failed at something. Close your eyes and imagine yourself back inside that moment. Journal below about how it felt:

_____

_____

_____

_____

Now rewrite that story, and imagine what it would be like if you had owned it. How would life change if you allowed yourself the space to be truly vulnerable? What would it take for you to become that woman?

_____

_____

_____

_____

So why doesn't this superpower come naturally to us? Why aren't we all able to just be vulnerable, lay it all out on the line, and not give a second thought about what anyone else thinks of us? Well, from a psychological standpoint, our fear of vulnerability all comes down to our fear of injury or getting hurt—even if that "injury" happens to be emotional. It's an instinct we have to protect ourselves as humans, and the idea of leaving ourselves open to potentially being hurt feels dangerous to us. But if we unpack this instinctual fear and really break it down, we can shift out of that nervous space and realize that many times, the only thing we have to fear is the fear itself.

A lot of my clients are entrepreneurs who promote and sell their products and services online and in person. The act of self-promotion can be a huge trigger for those who struggle with vulnerability. One of the biggest hurdles many of these women face is feeling comfortable putting themselves out there. They fear being rejected by potential clients, and they fear being ridiculed by their friends, families, and peers. I once worked with a woman who was terrified to announce on Facebook that she had begun working with a direct sales company. Though she was so excited for her new venture and wanted to share it with the world, she was nervous that she wouldn't be supported. She thought her friends might think she was involved in some sort of scam or not take her seriously. I asked her to tell me about the company she was working with, and why she chose it. I listened to her speak passionately about her new business for a good fifteen minutes. She raved about the company's mission statement, gushed about the team of amazing women she'd be working alongside, and told me how thrilled she was about all the opportunities ahead of her. Her excitement was palpable, and I could sense her pride as she described what this new journey meant to her. I asked her one very simple but powerful question after she stopped talking: What do you have to gain by keeping this major move quiet? Her answer? Nothing.

By keeping her new job a secret, she could be missing out on finding clients, connecting with others in her industry, or getting the support she so desperately wanted. And if none of that happened? That would be fine too. So what if someone thought she was involved in a pyramid scheme? Who cared if her neighbor's cousin's friend who she met once at a pool party thought she was making a mistake? The truth is, most people are so busy with their own lives that they really aren't paying much attention to your life. Isn't that kind of liberating? Most people really don't care about what you're doing. I know that may sound harsh, but it's the truth. And the people whose support should be meaningful to you are the ones who love and support you unconditionally, whether you're selling lipstick on the Internet, waiting tables at Waffle House, or working in the White House. Everyone else is just noise.

Our fear of being vulnerable is in our heads. It is a fear we actively choose by focusing on the worst-case scenario—and what we focus on expands. Most of the time, we're imagining scenarios in our minds that will never actually happen. We go to our default mode of fear and anxiety, assuming the worst. We get so caught up in being scared to put ourselves out there that we give up our ability to truly connect with others. We miss out on the opportunity to own our truth.

And you know what? Sometimes the worst does happen. Sometimes, someone says something nasty on your Facebook wall or to a mutual friend. Then what? Life goes on. Your business can still thrive. You can still thrive. We have to get out of the habit of living for other people's approval. We must stop holding ourselves back because we're afraid of being judged.

THE FEMININE EVOLUTION AND THE MAGIC OF SISTERHOOD

What if you're most afraid of being judged when you're around other women? As the popular saying goes, "Behind every successful woman is a tribe of other successful women who have her back." But that sisterhood sometimes eludes us. And it can be challenging to find women who *get it*. Rather than use the cliché that women are catty, competitive, or bitchy, let's unpack where that stereotype came from in the first place, shall we?

I don't think I've met one woman who hasn't gotten caught up in the vicious cycle of comparing herself to others—myself included. It is not just human nature to compete, but it is deeply baked within our feminine history to be favored, as a woman, based on our looks, status, or dowry. Back in the day, if you were the more beautiful woman, you got the man. If your family had the riches, you got the man. If your family was in a higher echelon, you got the man. And the man was the prize; he provided for you, gave you children, and made you "worthy." Women have been trained for centuries to beat out other women in order to climb the social ladder. Women have been bred, like horses, to compete.

Phew! Now you can take a breath. You're not crazy, and you certainly aren't alone if you have found yourself caught up in the insanity that is comparing, competing, and feeling jealous of another woman. I don't think we realize that our independence as women is still fairly new. It is only within recent years that women have gained the right to vote, been able to choose whom they want to marry (or not marry), determine their path in life, and make their own money. We are still working through our newfound liberation, and unfortunately many of us still remain chained to those antiquated ways of thinking.

But just as much as those qualities were part of our *her*story, so is our divine evolution. And women are evolving, every single day, by stepping into our power and upgrading our thoughts. Our independence has bred a brand new, fiercely unfuckwithable generation of confident, self-assured women who have learned to reprogram their minds. We now understand that while competition was once necessary for survival, sisterhood is now our lifeblood. Just like I wrote in my book *Girl Code*, collaboration beats competition, and women are better together. But how do you arrive at that empowered place when you are still doubting yourself? How do you show up as a bold, female leader when you are still protecting your own fragile ego?

One of the most common qualities of the evolved woman is that she does not allow feelings of comparison to swallow her whole. Of course, these feelings can sometimes appear, but an evolved woman recognizes them, works through them, and moves on.

These women are so in flow with who they are and so aligned with their authentic selves that the idea of stacking themselves up against anyone else is almost laughable. When you stand in your own power, competition dissolves. When you truly feel good about yourself, jealousy just isn't a thing. When you have mastered yourself, you naturally celebrate another woman: her beauty, her success, and her accomplishments. This is new thinking. This is female evolution. And this takes time.

One of the most effective (and most gratifying) ways to develop your confidence and move past the urge to compete is to lift another woman up. In fact, this is the first exercise I usually assign to a woman who is struggling with this issue. I know that this works, because it's something I practice constantly. And it doesn't need to be someone you know personally. With social media and the ease of the Internet, you can send an email or comment on someone's Instagram photo and offer kind, encouraging words of support within seconds. If being vulnerable is to lower your defenses, this is a brave way to do it. By reaching out to another woman, you level the playing field. Suddenly, she is no longer on the pedestal you once placed her on. Suddenly, you put yourself on her level and realize that we're all out here, trying to navigate our own feelings and do our best, day in and day out.

Sisterhood is one of the greatest things that can happen when you finally stop trying to pretend you're perfect. And sisterhood and success go hand in hand. While it's not impossible to achieve success in isolation, it sure is lonely. Finding a tribe of women to share your dreams with is one of the best ways to stay accountable to your work and create things inside a high vibration (a state of creativity, high energy, and gratitude). Masterminds, coaching workshops, networking events, even just an empowering and honest dinner can work like an IV of inspiration right to your soul. Giving and receiving support and love among other women is euphoric. And when you open yourself up to that kind of beauty, when you wholeheartedly speak your truth and let another woman in, you inspire others to do the same. You give women permission to unchain themselves from their old ways. You give women permission to love each other and, in turn, learn to love themselves.

My Facebook community is flooded with posts hourly from women who are so grateful that they finally have a place to come and share themselves. Whether it's celebrating a promotion at work, asking for advice on how to leave a broken marriage, or simply sharing a positive quote, my group provides women a safe space to learn the power of the sisterhood. It's truly an overwhelmingly wonderful thing to witness. I highly recommend joining my space, or finding something similar, to help illuminate your journey and remind you that there are people who want to see you win. Vulnerability brings the sisterhood together. The number one compliment I get from my readers and audience is "I love how vulnerable you are. I love that you are real and show us everything." Yet this is also the one thing my readers and audience struggle to achieve in their own lives. I think we love vulnerable people because they give us permission to dismiss perfection. I think we love to see people bare it all because it takes the pressure off. We get to take a breath. *Oh, see, she messed up and she's still going strong! Look, she lost a big client, and she's still an inspiration! She failed, and she lived to tell about it!*

As the infamous quote goes, "Once you've accepted your flaws, no one can use them against you." And that's very true. But let's take it a step further. Those flaws? They aren't flaws at all. They're human qualities that we all possess. Nobody is perfect. Nobody nails flawless presentations time and time again. Nobody avoids mistakes, judgment, or failures. And if they do, it's most likely because they're not out there trying a whole lot of things. They're remaining tucked deep inside their comfort zones, avoiding real growth. They are desperately protecting themselves from pain and, as a result, giving up the opportunity to experience joy. Because when you *do* live your life vulnerably, and you *do* wear your heart on your sleeve, you reap unimaginable rewards. You experience genuine connection with others, you get the chance to truly know yourself, and you build an unshakable sense of confidence that becomes very difficult to rattle.

In the space below, choose an area of your life where you'd like to become more vulnerable:

_____

_____

_____

_____

_____

What steps can you take to make that happen?

_____

_____

_____

_____

_____

POWER MANTRA

My ability to be vulnerable unlocks
a world of magic within me.

CHAPTER FIVE

Self-Love, Self-Sabotage, and Feeling Like a Fraud

A few months ago, I completed my fourth-ever ninety-minute SoulCycle challenge. It's exactly what it sounds like a SoulCycle class that lasts an hour and a half. Straight through, no breaks. *Intense* would be an understatement.

I did my first SoulCycle challenge back in 2015, the day after Thanksgiving, and believe it or not I breezed through it. I did the next one on New Year's Day, and that one was just as amazing. I actually remember thinking, *I could have stayed on that bike for another hour!* Surely aliens had invaded my body, because the old Cara would've been like *Fuuuuck that*. But things had changed. I was training for that moment. I was prepared, mentally and physically. And I truly couldn't believe how much I enjoyed the torture! The third ride was a few months later to celebrate the anniversary of a new SoulCycle studio, and once again, magic. But that last ride? A whole other story.

LIKE SHE OWNS THE PLACE

The weeks leading up to the class were rough. I was skirting the border of moderation and barely hanging on. I was working *hard*. During my time off, I celebrated my birthday twice, two Saturdays in a row, and then went to see two concerts the following week. Dinners out, lots of drinks, little sleep, with the icing on the cake being a four-day business trip to Atlanta, where I wined and dined my way through the entire city. Because it's not a business trip if you're not wining and dining your way through a new city, right? I returned to New York feeling like a prediabetic stuffed sausage who desperately needed a good night's sleep. You can only imagine my mental state when I clipped into that bike for that ninety-minute ride the day after I landed.

All of the scary thoughts were running through my mind before that class: *You've gained three pounds, which is now going to turn into ten! You know how this goes! You'll never be able to get back into your groove. You worked so hard to get where you are, and now you've ruined it forever. You are way too tired to do this class.* Ah, negative self-talk. Hello, old friend.

Logically, I knew how absurd all those thoughts were. Yet I chose them anyway. Then, during the class, I had the audacity to call my body a piece of shit. *A piece of shit.* Even though I chose to work out. Even though, despite my hectic schedule, I still showed up. Even though I put my health first. Still, I called my body a piece of shit. Why in the world would I say these things to myself?

The class started off just like any other. My instructor, Noa, has a great way of pacing us so we don't burn off all our energy right away. I felt really good throughout the first forty-five minutes. I made sure I slept well the night before, ate a power breakfast that morning, and hydrated. At about the forty-five-minute mark, though, I started to feel uncomfortable. Like, really uncomfortable. For starters, I was not on my usual bike, which sent my OCD self into a bit of a spiral. The room was unbearably warm because the class was so packed. As I grew more tired, I began to let all of those negative thoughts creep in. I felt the panic settle into my chest. My breath became harder to catch. I felt weak, which is not a feeling I love. I fell out of pace with the rest of the class, and that's when it happened. It went something like this: *What the hell is wrong with you? Why are you getting tired? Let's go, you piece of shit!*

Yikes. It freaked me out because, truthfully, I had not spoken to myself like that in quite some time. So why was it happening now? How could I call my body a piece of shit when I was working so hard? Why didn't I ever call my body a piece of shit when I was spending my entire Saturday at brunch drinking my body weight in mimosas? Why didn't I ever call my body a piece of shit when I canceled my workout at the last minute and decided to lounge on the couch and get lost in a *Keeping Up with the Kardashians* marathon instead? Why are we our harshest critics when we're trying to change for the better?

I'll tell you why: fear. Fear of feeling something entirely different. Fear of reaching past that comfort zone. Fear of maybe, *finally*, changing. The fact that I panicked on that bike is proof that something big was happening. It's proof that no matter how shitty I felt after all those birthday parties and late nights and giant hotel breakfasts and mini bottles of cheap wine on the plane, I still showed up. I showed up to be better. I showed up to be stronger. I showed up to honor my body and keep to my commitment. In the past, I would have just stayed in that spiral and kept eating and drinking, not willing to feel uncomfortable again by getting back on that bike. But things have changed. I refuse to be defeated by my own boring demons. I refuse to let my weakness overpower my strength. And I sure as hell refuse to allow myself to treat myself the way I did that Saturday afternoon in that dark, sweaty room ever again. Although I was doing something so good for myself, I was still kind of afraid of it.

I woke up the next morning, determined to approach my next class with self-compassion. Though I had let myself down the day before, I chose mindfulness. I chose to start fresh. I was tired, but I reminded myself that all I had to do was show up and do my best. There was no judgment, no competition. There was no name-calling allowed. The fact that I was there was more than enough. And guess what happened? I rode better that day than I had in weeks.

A funny thing happens when we start to intentionally speak to ourselves with love, when we take those few extra minutes to calm our nerves and to show ourselves some understanding. Think about the way we encourage children. Do we yell at them and tell them they suck? Do we bully them into succeeding? Of course not! We fill them up with love and support and tell them they can do anything. Don't you think it's time we start doing the same for ourselves?

SELF-LOVE IS A VERB

The idea of loving myself eluded me for most of my life. Self-love? What was that? You might as well have been speaking German to me. Fortunately, I never exactly *hated* myself, but the concept of self-love just wasn't on my radar. When I finally learned that confidence was impossible without self-love, my world was rattled in the best way possible.

I make a lot of fitness references when it comes to confidence, and it's because that's been the hardest thing for me to stick with. It's been the thing that doesn't come naturally to me, the thing that forces me to be patient with myself while continually pushing myself. It was a fitness class that helped me realize self-love is more than some pie-in-the-sky idea—it's a verb. A very intentional action. For me, self-love is not just speaking kindly to myself—it's making promises to myself and keeping them. Whether that's showing up to a workout class even when I'm not in the mood or writing that blog post even when I'm exhausted. Self-love is proving to myself I'm worthy of the things I really want to do, even when shit gets hard. Self-love is choosing myself, again and again, every day. Even when I don't like myself. Especially when I don't like myself.

Writing this book has been a massive act of self-love. This is the first time I'm working with a publisher, and as I mentioned in previous chapters, the heat is on. It's the first time I've had an entire company backing me up. The first time I've been pushed creatively. The first time someone else is holding me accountable to deadlines. It's taken an enormous amount of self-love to wipe away my tears of frustration (and there have been a few), to be disciplined with my time, and to fight the nagging feelings that I'm not enough. The act of writing and completing this book is an act of self-love. The act of doing my personal best and putting my anxiety to bed has been an act of self-love. The act of sometimes looking myself square in the face and saying, *Bitch, you've got this*, is an act of self-love.

If you're struggling with learning to love yourself, think about where you can take action in your life. Where can you start showing up for yourself? Where can you get really intentional? Where can you choose love over standing still?

Here's a simple yet powerful tool I use to remind myself that I am worthy of loving myself. I close my eyes and take six deep breaths. With each inhale, I imagine the words "I am enough" in glowing pink letters. Your letters may look different, but allow the phrase to remain the same. When I exhale, I imagine myself releasing any thoughts that do not serve me. After completing my breathing exercise, I let my breath return to normal, but I keep my eyes closed, and focus on visualizing the mantra. *I am enough.* Try this for ten minutes anytime you're feeling insecure, and see if it changes things for you. I have a feeling you might be very surprised at just how much it does.

THE WARS WE WAGE AGAINST OURSELVES

Be gentle. You're meeting parts of yourself you've
been at war with.
—UNKNOWN

I am no stranger to the weight-loss game. I've gained weight. I've lost weight. Do you know what happened to me once? I wrote a book in 2013 called *The Champagne Diet*, which is all about getting healthy, physically and emotionally. It's a story about how (I thought) I finally conquered my body image demons. It's not a diet book; it's a lifestyle guide to feeling and looking your best. The book came out, and then I went and gained more than thirty pounds. Thirty fucking pounds.

I now realize that was no accident. It was a result of keeping myself comfortably uncomfortable, at arm's length from my full potential. It was a way of keeping that warm blanket of safety wrapped tightly around me. It felt familiar to hold on to that extra weight. If I finally conquered my weight issues, what would be left to do?

Self-sabotage wears many different outfits, and none of them are designer. Some of us sabotage ourselves with relationships. Some of us do it with our careers. The most evident example of self-sabotage in my own life is my struggle with my weight. It did a number on my self-esteem until I took the time to figure out what was really going on.

Like I mentioned earlier, I started gaining weight in the second grade, right around the time my parents got divorced. Food quickly became my big, soft, cozy blanket, and I ate my feelings in the form of Chips Ahoy! and Doritos (vile, I know, but I was a child of the eighties). Food and I have always had a complicated relationship, and by the time I was thirty years old, I realized that maybe, just maybe, this was on purpose. I've never been obese, but I've always danced with an extra fifteen to twenty pounds that I couldn't quite shake for good. The way I looked controlled me. It's stalked my thoughts and ruled my self-esteem for most of my adult life.

My struggle with my weight isn't reflective of the way I've lived my life. I've been able to accomplish anything I set my mind to. Write a book? Done. Write six? No problem. Go on live television for the first time and totally slay it? Check. Why was I able to conquer all of my goals except to get to—and maintain—a healthy weight? What the hell was wrong with me?

I have come to understand through the years that the science of weight loss is easy. It's the emotional side that's the challenge. But I'm a master life coach. So why couldn't I master this? As Oprah said in a 2009 issue of *O* magazine, "I can't believe that after all these years, all the things I know how to do, I'm still talking about my weight." Ah, a kindred spirit if I've ever known one.

My struggle makes me think a lot about self-sabotage and the way it affects us as women. It makes me realize that so many of us are waging internal wars with our bodies and our minds. When I gained all that weight after *The Champagne Diet* came out, a lot of personal shit was going down in my life. I was deeply unhappy with my full-time job. I battled limiting beliefs about what I could or couldn't accomplish professionally. I was trying to be a new wife. I was trying to do it all, and I was *stressed*. Through the process of losing that weight (again), I realized that I can't overcome my self-sabotage unless I am loving myself in every area of my life.

Here is what those magazines that "celebrate" full-figured bodies won't tell you: It's not just about celebrating my curves and loving my body. It's about having the courage to face every single thing that's not working and address it. Most of all, it was about realizing that all along I hadn't been at war with my weight; I'd been at war with myself. And I was finally ready to wave the white flag.

In 2014, Jim Carrey gave a commencement speech to the Maharishi University of Management. He talked about the concept of choosing love over fear: "You can spend your whole life imagining ghosts, worrying about the pathway to the future, but all there will ever be is what's happening here and the decisions we make in this moment, which are based on either love or fear. So many of us choose our path out of fear disguised as practicality. What we really want seems impossibly out of reach and ridiculous to expect, so we never dare to ask the universe for it." How many times have you settled into self-sabotage because you were just too damn afraid to go after what you really wanted?

Maybe your self-sabotage looks different than mine. Or maybe it doesn't. But I urge you to examine the areas in your life where you're holding yourself back. What would you do if you weren't afraid? What would you do if you were willing to get uncomfortable? What would you do if you waved your own white flag and loved yourself enough to stop fighting against yourself?

ARE YOU COMFORTABLE OR ARE YOU HAPPY?

I will never forget the day I was promoted to director at MTV. I had been working hard at the company for years, and although it wasn't my ultimate dream to stay there, I refused to slack off or not do a good job. If my name is attached to something—anything—you bet your ass I'm working *my* ass off for it. My boss took notice of my hard work and I was suddenly a director, with a big fancy office, an expense account, and a team of twenty people. I remember everyone around me being so happy for me. "You did it!" And for a moment I thought, *I did it*. I was living the corporate dream. I had climbed the ladder and I was relishing the perks. I could have been content with that promotion and continued working hard to reach the next level of "success" within the company. I could have continued to collect my healthy paycheck and take my two-week vacation each year. But one major thing was missing: my happiness. During that time period a major question entered my mind: Am I happy, or am I comfortable? Whoa. Lightbulb moment. Don't the simplest of questions often have the most profound impact?

Before answering this, let's define happiness and how we cultivate it. There have been debates over whether happiness is a result of our choices or a choice in and of itself. I believe it's a choice, and we must choose it daily. But aren't we genetically predisposed to being happy or unhappy, you might ask? What about those with depression? Surely it must cancel out their ability to experience happiness regularly, right? Not necessarily. Studies show that our personal choices account for 40 to 50 percent of our happiness. Do you realize how much power that gives you? Martha Washington once said, "The greater part of our happiness or misery depends upon our dispositions, and not upon our circumstances." Research on happiness consistently shows that the happiest people do not have better life circumstances than those who are unhappy. They just have a better attitude. I do want to point out that depression is a serious condition, and I'm not minimizing it in any way. For some, it's not as easy as just thinking their way into a new mindset. But for many of us, we do have a choice. That choice requires some work, but it's a choice nonetheless.

It's natural to assume that being happy means being in a good mood all the time. It's actually the opposite. Studies show that striving to feel good every moment of every day may undermine your efforts to achieve happiness, because you'll never be satisfied. I see this as a common issue among women whom I deem "self-help junkies." People who become so obsessed with striving for positive mental health that it becomes unhealthy. Research reveals that an even-keeled, stable mood is more psychologically healthy than a mood in which you're constantly on a high.

Happiness is perspective. It's working toward fabulous things while being grateful for what you already have. Happiness is enjoying the journey and realizing that it's not a race to the end. Research suggests that happiness is a combination of how satisfied you are with your life and how good you feel on a day to day basis. It's about feeling fulfilled and excited about everything you have the power to create.

Comfort zones can masquerade as happiness, but they are anything but. Being comfortable may feel good temporarily, but if you're comfortable with remaining where you are and never striving to learn, grow, or take healthy risks, you're missing out on true happiness. Which, as I mentioned earlier, is all about creating your world.

Here are five ways to choose happiness now

Practice a gratitude ritual. Whether you reflect on what you're thankful for at the end of the day or when you wake up in the morning, be sure to think about what you appreciate in your life. Studies show that this not only boosts our mood but improves our physical health by lowering our blood pressure and improving our sleep.

Do something you love every day. Not all of us are able to pursue our passions through our careers, but we can still incorporate what we love into our everyday lives in some way. If you love writing, can you set aside thirty minutes a day to be creative? If you enjoy dancing, can you crank up your favorite playlist and spend fifteen minutes dancing in your living room before going to work? Own your time and fill it with the things you love.

Help others. Studies show that our happiness is strongly dependent on our relationships with others. Give back, be kind, and help those around you.

Move your body. Exercise releases endorphins, which are a natural happiness booster. Even twenty minutes a week can do wonders for your mood. And we all have twenty minutes to dedicate to being happy.

Visualize your ideal world. Clearly visualize what you want in your life. This paints a picture for your brain and helps you move toward your goals in a productive way. If you can see it, you can create it.

I urge you not to confuse comfort with happiness. Just because something feels good doesn't mean it's benefiting you. Check in with yourself daily. Are you striving toward all the things you desire? Or are you just accepting what's in front of you? You can be comfortably happy, but don't you dare allow yourself to live inside your comfort zone. You deserve so much more.

SELF-SABOTAGE IN A SUCCESS-OBSESSED WORLD

I will never forget the first time someone emailed me to tell me that one of my books had changed her life. I cross-checked the message so many times to make sure it was actually meant for me. *Could this be real?* I thought. Years later, I still sometimes wonder that, even after receiving hundreds, if not thousands, of messages from beautiful women who have been touched by my work.

Imposter syndrome describes high-achieving individuals who cannot internalize their accomplishments and constantly fear being exposed as frauds. "Despite external evidence of their competence, those exhibiting the syndrome remain convinced that they do not deserve the success they have achieved. Proof of success is dismissed as luck, timing, or as a result of deceiving others into thinking they are more intelligent and competent than they believe themselves to be."

Many women tell me they look up to me for being so positive and so inspiring, yet there are moments I look at myself and wonder what they're seeing. There are so many moments when I lose my shit, cry from being overwhelmed, or lack motivation that it's difficult for me to accept that I could be any kind of role model for anyone. There are so many moments when I'm not my best self, and I fear that if I were "exposed" to any of my readers, they might run the other way.

And I am not alone. I hear from my clients and readers all the time about how they feel like they're going to be "found out" by their employers or their peers. Whether it's not allowing themselves to be joyful about a promotion because they don't feel qualified or feeling too young or too old to be in a certain position, so many women struggle with feeling like they just don't belong where they are. It happens across the board, at all ages, in all levels of experience.

This is not a new phenomenon, either. In the 1970s, Oberlin College psychology professor Pauline Rose Clance noticed that a large number of her incredibly accomplished students all had something in common: They didn't feel they deserved success. Clance could relate, as she had gone through the exact same experience in grad school. Curious, she and her colleague Suzanne Imes began interviewing these women and eventually wrote up their findings in a paper called "The Imposter Phenomenon in High Achieving

Women." Their initial findings indicated that women were predisposed to the imposter phenomenon, "since success for women is contraindicated by societal expectations and their own internalized self-evaluations." Since that research, it's actually been proven that nearly everyone, both men and women, experiences imposter syndrome, although it's not proven to be a psychological syndrome at all. Both men and women, from all walks of life and all professional backgrounds, often feel that they are undeserving of their success. However, according to Clance, women are more vocal about that feeling. The good news is that feeling like an imposter is totally normal, and it is something you can work through. "Many people can live with it, and it changes as they get experience in a job," says Clance. "Often knowing that a lot of other people experience it is helpful."

Here's a reassuring truth: Nearly every single person on this planet has doubted themselves at some point. In fact, according to the *International Journal of Behavioral Science*, 70 percent of people experience imposter syndrome. I've spoken to some of the most successful women I know, and nearly every single one of them has questioned her own worth. Even the most confident women struggle with it, and it doesn't go away after achieving higher levels of success. In fact, it happens more often. As the saying goes, "With every level comes a new devil." There are new challenges, new players, and bigger stakes involved as you accomplish more in your career and in your life. Imposter syndrome is totally normal. The difference between those who choose confidence over imposterism? They keep fucking going. They carry on, even when they feel like a fraud. They charge ahead, even when they feel out of place.

LIKE SHE OWNS THE PLACE

They believe in themselves, even when they have to cross-check that email to make sure it was really meant for them.

I did a quick survey about imposter syndrome in my Facebook group, and here are some of the comments I received:

OH YES. I'm twenty-three and three years into my professional career. I feel as if every week I have a flash of imposter syndrome. A lot of it has to do with contributing factors like having lots of responsibility but still facing the "oh but you're so young" stuff in the workplace, or not getting compensated accordingly. I have to remind myself that I'm where I am for a reason, I work my ass off every single day and night (as I write this from my office still), but sometimes it's still hard to remember that I belong here in this professional space.

I've just started working with people with disabilities. I feel like I run from one problem to the next, and I've been given compliments about how calm and friendly I am being. . . . All the while I feel like a stressed-out chicken being pulled in all directions. I mean, me? Really? I am doubting myself so much.

YES! I have experienced this in the past. I worked SO hard to get to a job that I loved but I was always waiting for someone to cry "fraud," or whenever I was presenting or chair of a committee, it was a feeling of waiting for the other shoe to drop and for someone to find out I didn't really belong. And yet, I have the degrees. I have the experience but it didn't seem to quell the feeling. I felt like, if I just made myself visible enough and on enough committees, that I would belong and no one would call me out as a fraud. Entering into a new career and going through law school now, I can feel that familiar anxiety rising up again. I ask myself at least once a week why I'm in law school. Should I even be here? Can I do this? Being surrounded by others who seem to be made for this and I question myself. I also tell myself, I deserve to be here. I earned my way here. No one gave me this. Even with that pep talk, there is still a small voice that says, "fraud."

God yes, last year it made me so stressed and ill. I was convinced I wasn't as good as some other writers with my publishers. I kept waiting for an email to say sorry, we made a mistake. It never came thankfully. Sales have been pretty good, reviews were good (most of them), and I've stopped comparing myself to the others, most of the time. The doubt still creeps in now and again.

Those comments, along with more than a hundred more, remind me that we're all in the same boat when it comes to feeling out of place at times. But it doesn't have to be a negative experience. I now see it as a sign that I'm leveling up, that I'm entering new territory and expanding. Growth is uncomfortable at times. If you're remaining in your comfort zone, you're not doing much of anything. If you're never testing your abilities, pushing your own boundaries, or challenging yourself, you just aren't evolving. And if you're not evolving, it's impossible to gain confidence. Have you ever heard someone talk about how much they learned about themselves by doing the same exact thing for forty years? We've got to change. We've got to feel awkward about it at times, and we've got to be okay with that.

S o what's a gal to do if she's feeling like a big fat fraud? There are ways to tackle imposter syndrome, ways to pump yourself up and remind yourself that you are not, in fact, a fraud, and you deserve to be exactly where you are. Aside from the perhaps obvious, like remembering just how badass you are and listing all the incredible things you've accomplished, one of my colleagues, life and business coach Desiree Wiercyski, suggests playing out what it would be like if an actual imposter were doing the things you're doing. Imagine someone without your talent, your drive, your passion, and your experience stepping into your life for a day. How's that for a reality check?

And my absolute favorite way to handle it? Simply own it. Walking in your truth, being vulnerable, and being honest with yourself and others. I can't tell you how many women I've admitted feelings of imposterism to, only to be met with the biggest

> **TIP:** Keep a love letter stash. I collect positive emails and take screenshots of social media comments I receive from women that remind me I'm doing a great job. It's tough to believe you're an imposter if you have an overflowing collection of compliments from others who believe in you!

sigh of relief I've ever heard. We are all in this together. Sometimes knowing that is enough.

BELIEVE IT, THEN BE IT

Before leaving my job at MTV, I spent a lot of time envisioning my future. Each morning, I'd wake up and picture my ideal day playing out in my mind, even though I wasn't quite there yet. I'd imagine, in vivid detail, how I'd spend my day when I was finally free from my day job, living in my ideal world. That fantasy helped me keep the momentum going when I was trudging through rush-hour traffic and trying to muster the energy to make it through mind-numbing meetings and long, stressful days, praying for the moment I could kiss that all good-bye.

But things really got interesting when I finally did leave MTV and was living in my ideal world. I believed it, and I was being it. And it did not come without bouts of anxiety and self-doubt. In the afterglow of my resignation, I started to grasp that there was no direct deposit happening in two weeks. I started to grasp that my success was no longer going to be evaluated by an HR department. It was all on me. It was showtime, and I had to believe more than ever. And believe I did.

Something magical happens when you pull the trigger on your future: You uncover parts of yourself that you didn't know were there. You tap into a wealth of creativity, energy, and hustle that had been lying dormant among your fears. You show up in a big way. You change your entire life.

A lot of people are fans of the "fake it till you make it" ap-

Here's how you can apply the "believe it, then be it" approach to your world:

Celebrate your talents. It's time to give yourself some serious props. We spend so much time beating ourselves up, obsessing over what we are lacking, but that gets us nowhere. Celebrate your strengths and the things that make you powerful. Incorporate these talents into your world every single day. Are you really great at making people feel good about themselves? Do more of that. Are you a fantastic writer? Start that blog you've been dreaming about. The more you focus on what you're great at, the faster you'll build your self-esteem.

Put your weaknesses to bed. On the flip side, it's time to let go of the things you may not feel as strong in. This doesn't mean you shouldn't strive to expand your skill set, but if you really struggle with certain things, forget them and move on. For example, I'm not the best at math. It doesn't come naturally to me, even with years of practice. I've now learned to offload the analytical side of my business to someone who can do a better job at it. I play up my strengths and delegate the rest.

Crown yourself. Do you know how many years it took me to call myself an author? Do you know how uncomfortable I felt when someone else called me an author? Even though I had published multiple books and topped best-seller lists. Even though I had five-star reviews and readers around the world who were enjoying my work. That's imposter syndrome for you. But the more you begin using words and terms to describe yourself as the woman you are, the sooner you'll step into that role. Let's say you just launched your graphic design business, but you don't have one client yet; you must call yourself a designer. Just hit publish on your first blog post? Congrats! You're now a blogger. Anoint yourself. You are worthy. A great way to do this is by updating your LinkedIn profile or posting it on Facebook or somewhere the public will see it. The sooner you can put it out there to an audience, the sooner you will feel it.

Step into action. I've talked about action a lot throughout this book, and there's a reason for it. The more we're in motion, the less we feel stuck. When we are actively pursuing our dreams and goals, no matter how small those steps are, we simply don't have the time to ruminate on our fears or shortcomings. Create actionable steps each week to help you build your confidence and live the life you want to live.

proach, but that's not where real confidence is born. Faking something implies you don't believe it. Faking something implies you don't have what you need, in this exact moment, to be your best self. That's untrue. Rather than faking it till you make it, I encourage women to "believe it and then be it." This is my favorite part of self-reinvention, the most exhilarating place to begin when creating a new vision for your life. Get into the *feeling* of being who you want to be. Believe it with every ounce of your soul. Then get out there and just start getting into action.

———

n the space below, I invite you to think about an area of your life where you feel like an imposter.

———

———

———

———

How can you start believing in yourself?

———

———

———

———

POWER MANTRA

I choose love over fear. I show up for myself
and trust that I have everything I need.

CHAPTER SIX

Audacious Auditing

Evolving involves eliminating.

—ERYKAH BADU

f you've ever felt like your life was spinning out of control, then you know exactly what it feels like to be anything *but* confident. Whether it was a family member who knew no boundaries, your own negative thought patterns, an abusive boss, or a shitty boyfriend who made you second-guess your sanity, many of us have found ourselves in situations where we have felt lost and hopeless. Living confidently requires a term I call *Audacious Auditing*: the process of reviewing and removing negative people, habits, things, and thoughts that do not serve us—and doing it all without guilt. In this chapter, you'll learn how and why it's crucial that you do a major life audit to preserve your happiness and peace of mind and build your self-worth.

AUDITING YOUR CIRCLE

Guard your time fiercely. Be generous with it, but intentional about it.
—DAVID DUCHEMIN

Jim Rohn once famously said that we are the average of the five people we spend the most time with. If you just cringed, then read on, sister. It's true that the people we spend time with influence us: both positively and negatively. I want you to take a moment and think about your inner circle—the people you speak to and see the most. What kind of people are they? How do they make you feel? What are your conversations like? Most importantly, when you engage with them, do you feel energized or do you feel drained?

If everyone in your life is great and inspiring and supportive, then you're very fortunate. Feel free to skip this section and move on to the next. But if you're like most of us, this isn't the case. Many of us are so used to the people in our lives that we never think to take stock of who they are and what they offer us emotionally. We are so conditioned to accept old friends and family members that we let their subpar behavior slide and wonder why we're always in a bad mood when we talk to them. We accept insults, drama, and negativity because "that's just how they are." We never stop to think, *Hey, I don't need this person's poison in my life! I deserve more.*

Sometimes it's difficult to know what defines a "toxic" person. That term is used often, so let's take a moment to clarify what it actually means. I've come to understand that not everyone in my life is going to be as peaceful, happy, or optimistic as I am. And that's fine. I have been able to accept those people for who they are, and I understand the limitations of the types of conversations I can have with them. However, certain people who have come into my life have been downright toxic. We're going to discuss both types in this chapter, but let's start with the most dangerous people: the toxic ones. I categorize toxic people as ones who make me question my self-worth, who try to take advantage of my kindness and generosity, who deplete my energy, or who try to sabotage or control me. Toxic people will bring out the worst in you, causing you to react in ways that are out of character. You must either remove them from your life completely or set clear boundaries for them in order to protect yourself.

I once had a client who was a stay-at-home mom building a home-based business. After her children entered high school, she decided it was time to create something for herself. Her husband was constantly questioning her motives, claiming she was trying to gain independence to finally leave him. Though she said he'd always been controlling and degrading, things escalated greatly when she began working. She desperately wanted to pursue her passion, make her own money, and feel like she had a purpose again, but this man made it challenging, to say the least. Every day, he'd tell her she was stupid and incapable, and he referred to her business as a joke. It broke my heart to learn he treated her this way and to see her so disempowered by his behavior. Her husband was toxic, harming her self-esteem and doing major damage to her psyche. Through our work together, I encouraged her to create a mental toolbox to guard herself and set new bound-aries in the marriage.

The first step was protecting herself and her spirit. I encouraged her to create positive affirmations that she read each morning and kept handy whenever he went on a tirade to help her calm down. Repeating phrases like "I am strong, I am valued, and I am loved" helped her remember that the way her husband treated her had nothing to do with her and reminded her that she had a strong support system around her. We also made sure she kept in close contact with friends and family who knew her situation. Being open and honest about a toxic relationship is crucial. This is no time to feel embarrassed. Your friends and family love you and want to see you happy. Even if you confide in one or two people, it makes all the difference to know you are not alone.

Another important—arguably the *most* important—step she took was to disengage and not feed into his behavior. Whenever he insulted her, she calmly told him she felt disrespected and would no longer allow him to speak to her that way, and she left the room. Sometimes physically walking away can shift the en-ergy of the situation and give you room to breathe and gain per-spective on what's happening. Although it's our instinct to defend ourselves or argue with a toxic person, that only fuels their fire.

And finally, don't be scared to seek professional help. My cli-ent came to me when she needed help most, and the work we did together strengthened her and made her able to confidently han-dle her situation. In addition to working with me, I encouraged her to find a therapist in her area to work with in tandem to help manage her situation. Whether it's a life coach, a therapist, or a domestic violence hotline, help is available to you, and you do not have to remain in a situation that is dangerous to you physically or emotionally.

It can be exceedingly difficult to cut out toxic people—especially when they happen to be family members or significant others. Believe it or not, after months and months of hard work on herself, my client stayed with her husband. Auditing your circle is *really* challenging. It requires a deep love for yourself and an unwavering dedication to your own self-esteem. And it can be especially hard for a sensitive and empathetic person. (Do you see me waving my hand in the air?)

My client wasn't the first experience I had with a toxic relationship. I dated someone for a long time who was emotionally abusive toward me. Perhaps that's why I have so much empathy for women in these situations. My ex would look for ways to play on my insecurity over my weight and try to tear me down whenever he had the chance. I remember being with him at a restaurant one night and ordering a cheeseburger. He looked directly at my body, his eyes scanning me from head to toe, and said, "Are you sure about that?" I was mortified. One Halloween as we were getting ready for a party, I came out of the bedroom in my costume and his mood shifted instantly. He became annoyed with me and demanded I change because I looked too fat in the shorts I had on. He also once told me he would propose to me if I lost thirty pounds.

Sharing all of this with you honestly makes me go, *What the hell, Cara?* But believe me when I tell you, I certainly didn't seek out someone who tore me down from the first date. Manipulation is a slow and subtle process, and in my case, I didn't even realize it until it was in full swing. I met my ex when I was twenty-one years old, and I hadn't a clue what it meant to be empowered at that point in my life. I was still finding myself as a woman, and consequently the type of man I was drawn to was a reflection of that search. My ex was mysterious, dominant, and incredibly charismatic. And I was hooked from the start.

I spent the first few years of that relationship chasing after him the way you do a rowdy puppy. Every so often I'd clutch him in my arms and he'd allow me to keep him close, but in a few moments, he'd become restless and I'd find him running all over town. I never had a chance to see his true colors, because I barely had a chance to spend much time with him at all. The beginning of our relationship was pretty tumultuous, to say the least.

We didn't get serious until a few years later, and at that point I believe he committed because I had given him an ultimatum. I broke up with him because I had grown tired of the madness, and he came back with the grand gesture: "Let's move in together." I was beyond thrilled, until I began to experience all the behavior mentioned earlier: the control, the jealousy, the insults, and the manipulation. Perhaps he resented me for finally pinning him down; perhaps he had been this way all along. Either way, I was five years deep into the relationship by the time it reached its pinnacle of toxicity, and I was just as terrified to leave as I was to stay.

Eventually, I sought professional help because I could no longer handle the emotional torture. And the biggest shocker for me was that my therapy sessions didn't focus on him at all. Instead, we explored why *I* chose to remain with a man who treated me so poorly. It took me years—and a hell of a lot of internal work—to realize I was being mistreated. When you're in the throes of it, it can be challenging to separate yourself from the situation. Insanity becomes the new norm. Disrespect becomes the new norm. You begin to think you deserve what you are getting. You begin to think you are the problem. I'm so grateful I got the help I needed, because the best choice I ever made was to love myself enough to leave that relationship.

I also want to make it clear that I've moved on from the pain of that relationship and even forgiven my ex for his behavior. I never did get an apology, but sometimes you have to accept the apologies you never received. I have a much clearer understanding of the entire dynamic now: who he was at the time, who I was at the time, and how it became the perfect storm for a painful yet crucial period of my life. What I learned about myself in that relationship paved the way for my expansion, my confidence, and my place in the world.

Not every person who has a negative impact on you is necessarily toxic. When it comes to the more melodramatic types, you may not need as drastic an approach. Melodramatic people aren't as dangerous as toxic people, but they certainly aren't fun to be around. These people love to create drama, stir the pot, and drain you spiritually and energetically. It's important to distance yourself from these people, and here's one way to do it: Every time you speak to that person, *shift the conversation*. Let's take someone who loves drama, for example. We all know that one person who fixates on either their own or everyone else's problems. They call you to give you the play-by-play on every single bad thing that's happening in their world, or to gossip about everyone else's problems. The next time they try to suck you dry with the same old story, try to get them to focus on the solution. Ask them point blank: *How can we solve this problem?* Dramatic people thrive on theatrics. They don't want their problems to end. They want to remain steeped in the bullshit. So when you consistently try to get them to focus on a solution, either they'll be on board and you'll wind up helping them (which is a win), or they'll move on to the next person who will participate in their performance.

Although those kinds of melodramatic people are certainly unhealthy to be around, what's worse are people who intentionally try to hurt you. If you have someone in your life who hurls insults at you—or gives those infuriating backhanded compliments—I've found it helpful to call them out on their behavior. The next time that person says something rude or pointed, ask them if they are aware of what they're doing. Let them know they are making you feel bad. A simple statement like, "Do you know when you say X, you really hurt my feelings?" is perfect. Then give them a moment to process what you've just said. At that point, it's important to let them know you've set a new boundary, which no longer allows for you to be abused, and you need to end the conversation. Honesty is the best policy, even for those of us who cringe at the thought of confrontation. Think about it this way: Isn't it easier to feel uncomfortable for a few minutes rather than feel uncomfortable every single time you speak to that person?

I once had a colleague who loved gossip. She took every opportunity to text and call me with a new story about various women in our industry. The first few times she exhibited her catty behavior I was stunned. I didn't know her that well, and I was quickly learning that she was not the kind of woman I wanted to let into my circle. I listened at first, and I felt extremely uncomfortable after those conversations. I'm a girl's girl and I *hate* talking shit. I decided that I wanted to distance myself from her, and my new plan was to exit any conversations we had that included gossip. Sure enough, she called me over Christmastime last year and jumped right into one of her stories. "I'd rather talk about something positive today," I told her. The silence was deafening. Within minutes, our phone call ended, and I've barely spoken to her since. Confidently setting boundaries will allow you to feel better about who you are and what you allow in your world. And as I always say, there is no time for bullshit when you're building an empire.

And if you're worried about offending people by cutting them out of your life, remember this: You can be kind *and* confident. Setting boundaries is not selfish; it's a method of survival. If someone is offended by your decision to protect your spirit, then that's on them.

Here's your cheat sheet on how to handle toxic and/or drama-loving people:

Toxic Person Response Protocol

Step 1. Protect yourself. Create positive affirmations that build your self-esteem, focus on self-care, and confide in friends or family to let them know you're in a toxic relationship.

Step 2. Create a boundary and make them aware of it. Design a power statement like, "I am no longer available to be disrespected by you" and let the toxic person know when they cross a boundary.

Step 3. Seek professional help. Find a local therapist or life coach, or contact a domestic violence hotline. You don't have to suffer alone, and there is a way out.

Drama Lover Response Protocol

Step 1. Shift the conversation. The next time you find yourself in a conversation centered on negativity or drama, shift it by challenging that person to find a solution. Or, if you find yourself in a conversation centered on gossip, let that person know you are no longer available for that type of discussion.

Step 2. Create a boundary and make them aware of it. Design a power statement like, "I am no longer available for conversations that drain me," and let it be known the next time you find yourself there.

Step 3. Exit the conversation. Politely let that person know you need to hang up the phone, or stop talking. A simple reminder of your power statement works to reiterate the fact that you refuse to engage in that kind of behavior.

n the space below, identify the toxic people in your life.

_____

_____

_____

_____

How do these people help your confidence?

_____

_____

_____

_____

How do these people harm your confidence?

_____

_____

_____

CREATING POWER CIRCLES

The other night I had dinner with a few of the women I met through my SoulCycle class. I became friendly with these girls by chatting with them before class over the course of a few months, and we finally decided it was time to get together. The four of us arrived at dinner and were so wrapped up in such great conversation that the waiter came over three times to see if we were ready to order. We hadn't even looked at the menu! We talked about things like our careers, feminism, body image, sex, friendships, and love. Nearly four hours later, we realized we had basically shut down the restaurant.

"Do you realize we did not talk badly about anyone tonight?" I asked them. This is always such a breath of fresh air for me because, unfortunately, many women go there. But we actively sought each other out because all of us were seeking female friendships that are all about good vibes and support. We'd rather talk about our dreams than other people. I walked away from that dinner feeling refreshed, inspired, and confident. We toasted that night to the start of a long friendship.

I should also mention that our positive conversation was not devoid of messy, vulnerable realness. We all opened up that night about our struggles and our fears. We talked candidly about the things we feel challenged by in our lives, and that's what made our night so magical. For every honest admission, one of us jumped in to offer support, lend advice, or just be an ear. For every truth brought to the table, there was zero judgment. Being around positive people does not mean all conversations are sunshine and rainbows. Choosing happiness does not mean choosing delusion. There is a stark difference between honesty and negativity. Creating true and powerful friendships means dropping the facades and allowing yourself to be vulnerable. If you're surrounding yourself with women (or men) who are pretending everything is perfect, you'll find yourself feeling very alone.

Supportive, positive people will push you to be better, not point out your flaws. They will listen to you without judging you. They will celebrate your success and be a shoulder to lean on when you stumble. They will challenge you to be the best version of yourself, while reminding you that you're perfect exactly as you are.

Find your tribe. They are out there. You are not stuck with or limited to the people around you by default. You can create brand-new friendships and sisterhoods at any age. In fact, I think it's better to find new friendships as we get older because we have a sense of who we are, without all the insecurity that comes with youth. Seek out opportunities to meet like-minded women at places you love to go. Whether it's a fitness class, a book club, or a networking event, women just like you are out there, and they're looking for healthy connection just like you are.

Facebook groups can be a great tool for finding new friends. In fact, in my Facebook community, the Slay Baby Collective,

I've watched women from all over the world form real friendships that go beyond the computer. I started the group because I felt isolated. I knew if I felt that way, other women did too. I wanted to create a safe space where women could share their dreams, ideas, and thoughts with other like-minded women. We now have close to ten thousand members (and growing!) who actively engage in the group every day. Many of the girls meet offline as well, and have monthly meet-ups in their local areas where they get coffee, drinks, or dinner. I try to host a few meet-ups per year in different cities to bring these women together in person. It's a beautiful thing to witness people connect, especially when they've been so hungry for that experience. The more you fill your life with people who lift you up and energize you, the less space you have for those who drain you.

And don't be scared to ask someone out on a girl date! Just like in romantic dating, most people are nervous to make the first move. If you're clicking with someone, invite them to hang out. Don't be afraid of rejection, and don't cancel out of fear. Show up with an open heart and an open mind. As the popular saying goes, strangers are just friends you haven't met yet. Some of those strangers may wind up changing your whole world.

SUPERCHARGE YOUR SELF-TALK

Another thing you may need to audaciously audit? The negative chatter in your own head. In the past week, have you said something bad about your body, your business, your looks, or any area of your life? In the past week, have you called yourself crazy, fat, or stupid? That sounds harsh, but even the things we say in jest affect the way we think about ourselves. It's not just the way the people around us speak to us that matters; the way we speak to *ourselves* has a profound impact on our self-esteem. Even when we think we're being silly or self-deprecating, it's incredibly harmful to call ourselves names or take jabs at our own character.

We must be mindful of the way we talk to ourselves, because we're listening.

Most of us are programmed to think negatively. We replay negative thoughts in our minds that are often rooted in our childhood. For example, if you grew up hearing your family members tell you, "You'll never amount to anything," you will probably wind up believing that as an adult. That belief will continue to resurface and manifest in various areas of your life. You'll feel insecure, unworthy, and incapable of being successful until you rewire your mind to think a new, positive thought about yourself. That's the good news about all of this—you can completely shift your thinking into a space of positivity, self-love, and confidence. You have the power to totally reprogram your mind to make it work *for* you rather than against you, and help you feel fantastic.

If you struggle with positive self-talk, think about reframing the way you address yourself. Some research has found that it's not just about *what* we say to ourselves, but *how* we say it. One

2014 report describes the role of language in self-talk and suggests that when practicing it, don't refer to yourself in the first person, such as *I* or *me*. Instead, refer to yourself in the second or third person (using *you, he,* or *she*) or refer to yourself by name. I usually choose something playful when practicing my own self-talk, and say things like, "You look good, boo!" or "You got this, babe!" It makes me smile, and it helps it feel more lighthearted and less self-helpy. The study also suggests that using second or third person in self-talk can help you think more objectively about your response and emotions, as well as help reduce stress and anxiety.

You may have heard the power phrase "Change your thoughts, change your life," and it is the truth. Affirmations are powerful words and phrases that help guide your thoughts and strengthen the connection between the conscious and subconscious mind. They are one of the best tools for building confidence and staying in a positive and high-energy space. Here's a trick when changing your thoughts: Rather than trying to obsessively eliminate the negative ones, focus on incorporating more positive ones. Eventually, you'll flood your mind with so much goodness that the bullshit will fade out.

I'll be the first to admit: I always thought affirmations were cheesy at best. I assumed they were meaningless phrases self-help junkies said in the mirror every morning, and a cool girl like me just wasn't interested. Boy, was I wrong. I'm now obsessed with them; in fact, I write new ones almost every day. By repeating phrases like the ones that follow, you can boost your mood, create more self-awareness, improve your health, and ultimately live a more empowered life.

Take a moment and think about your self-talk. What is currently playing on a loop in your mind? I'll tell you what's circling around in my head: I've been struggling with writer's block

> Here are some of my go-to phrases. You can use these when you wake up in the morning, before you go to bed at night, or any time you want to give yourself a little boost. I should add that you've got to do more than just say these words. You've got to *feel* them, with your body. You have to visualize them—imagine they are true, and what implications their truth has in your life. Only if you do the hard work of really believing them, in the moment, will they materialize.
>
> Today I wake up filled with gratitude and light.
>
> I am so excited about what this day will bring and all the opportunities I am about to create.
>
> I begin my day with clarity, confidence, and faith.
>
> I feel healthy, sexy, strong, and beautiful in my body.
>
> I get to choose the woman I want to be today.
>
> I feel grounded and centered today.
>
> Today I get to give love and spread positivity to those around me. I get to make people's lives a little better.
>
> I always make the best decisions by listening to my intuition.
>
> I am always guided and I know that what is for me will not pass me.

throughout much of the process of writing this book. Although this is my seventh book, I've been telling myself that my work isn't good enough and may not be taken seriously. Whoa! Why would someone with so much training, experience, and practice in self-awareness still struggle with this? Because we're all human. We *all* experience feelings of self-doubt. We all deal with imposter syndrome, and we all say some really horrible things to ourselves. The trick is identifying and catching the pattern before it spreads. Thoughts, especially the bad ones, tend to go viral in our minds. Think them enough and they become that catchy song that you can't get out of your head. And the song is *not* a good one.

Here's a great exercise to help you replace those disempowering thoughts with new, affirming ones that build your confidence. Every time you think a harmful thought about yourself, search for a truth to oppose it. For example, when I think to myself, *My work isn't good enough to be taken seriously,* I can replace it with *My books are best-sellers that have helped change women's lives around the world.* The difference between those two statements is incredibly powerful. If I chose the former statement every day, I'd get nothing done. However, if I chose the latter, which is my truth, I'd become unstoppable. Can you guess which I'm choosing to power through this writing process?

Write down some of the negative things you tell yourself regularly.

_____

_____

_____

_____

_____

Now replace those thoughts with your truth.

_____

_____

_____

_____

THE HABIT HACK

A major part of developing confidence is eliminating the habits that do not serve us. Whether it's overeating, overdrinking, sleeping around, or not sleeping enough, we all have our vices. It's time to take an inventory of our daily routine and regular habits and cut out anything that makes us feel less than fabulous. It's also important to create what I call *success rituals* that empower us and support our self-worth.

According to *New York Times* business writer and author Charles Duhigg, every habit starts with a three-part process: a psychological pattern called a *habit loop*. First, there's a cue that tells your brain to go into automatic mode and let a behavior unfold.

"Then there's the routine, which is the behavior itself. That's what we think about when we think about habits," Duhigg says. The third step is the reward—something that your brain likes that helps it remember the "habit loop" in the future and come back to it again and again. For example, I have a habit of mindlessly eating potato chips while working at my desk. The cue for me is when I sit down at my laptop and open up my email. The routine is eating the chips. And the reward is that feeling of having something to munch on while I handle a mundane task.

As soon as a behavior becomes automatic, the decision-making part of your brain goes into a kind of sleep mode. "The brain starts working less and less. The brain can almost completely shut down. And this is a real advantage, because it means you have all of this mental activity you can devote to something else," says Duhigg. Now, all of that's great if you're working to develop a new, healthy habit. But what happens when we've got a few unhealthy habits under our belt like those "email chips"? We're literally not thinking about anything in those moments. We're just doing. And that's kind of scary.

I love to drink wine. In my opinion, there's nothing better than ending a busy day with a big, beautiful glass of red. For the longest time, my nightly habit involved shutting down my computer around seven in the evening, lighting all my candles, and pouring that glass (the cue). It was my "shutoff"—my reward after a hard day's work. Pretty quickly, that nightly glass became two. And then three. Before I knew it, I was drinking more than half a bottle of wine per night—sometimes more. And it was totally habitual—my routine. Although I enjoyed that downtime at night, other areas of my life were suffering as a result. My sleep became interrupted, and I often woke up groggy the next day. I started bailing out of my workouts because I felt drained from the night before. I put on a few pounds and felt bloated. Soon enough, all of those things added up and I felt my confidence slipping away before my very eyes. My "reward" wasn't much of a reward at all anymore.

I'll never forget the day I realized my evening wine habit had become an issue. One of my readers mentioned that I hadn't shown my face on social media in a long time. She sent me a message asking if everything was okay. Because I run my business online, it's important for me to personally engage with my readers via Instagram and Facebook videos and photos. I love hopping on my social media channels and talking to my audience and showing them that there's a real person behind my books and words. I took a look back at the previous few weeks and realized she was right—I had not shown my face. And it was because I wasn't feeling confident.

I immediately whipped out a piece of paper and made a list of all the things that made me feel good, or "high vibe" as I like to call it. I asked myself when I felt my best, when I had the most energy, and when I enjoyed showing up for my audience most. One of the perks of being a trained life coach? Knowing how—and when—you need to coach yourself. The answer was evident in my first line: "When I'm not drinking regularly." I knew I had to change my habit in order to support my best self. And just like that, I did. You know what? Cutting it out was so much easier than I had anticipated. I focused on the end result—what I knew

I'd gain from curbing that nightly habit. I focused on how I wanted to feel, which was healthier, sharper, well rested, fresh-faced, and more self-assured. Rather than thinking about "giving up" the wine, I thought about everything I had to gain. It's really important to adopt a mind-set of gift giving when you cut a bad habit out of your life.

Part of the gift I gave myself involved replacing my negative habit with a positive one, or creating a new *success ritual*. I knew I still wanted an experience in the evening that would help me detach from my work and unwind. I wanted to celebrate the end of a long day in a healthy and productive way. So I began drinking herbal tea—a blend that promotes restful sleep. Now, at around seven in the evening, I still close my laptop and light my candles, but instead of pouring my wine, I pour a cup of tea (most nights). I set an intention to relax and I enjoy my night. I love making my tea ritual feel fancy, so I use vintage teacups and sometimes even light a stick of incense. Of course, some nights I still enjoy a glass of wine or two. It's all about balance, and understanding that the habitual actions are the ones that count the most—so I make sure that the things I'm doing on a regular basis are healthy, confidence-boosting routines that will ultimately make me feel great.

Maybe it's not the wine for you—but the food. Maybe you've gotten into the habit of grabbing fast food at night because you're too tired to cook a nutritious dinner. Or maybe you're stress-eating cookies during the afternoon while meeting last-minute deadlines at work. Or maybe you're staying up late and not getting enough sleep to feel rejuvenated. I invite you to take a good, hard

Here are some examples of common unhealthy habits and some more positive habits to replace them with:

Grabbing a cookie with your afternoon coffee. Instead of reaching for the cookie or sweet treat, try having a banana instead. Remind yourself that the banana will provide sustainable energy, and while the cookie may taste great in the moment, it will ultimately cause a sugar crash. Knowing you made the healthier choice will help you feel more confident in the way you treat your body.

Skipping your morning workout because you're too busy. Although it may seem tempting to give yourself that extra hour in the morning to work rather than exercise, reminding yourself that the exercise will provide you with an endorphin rush, which will boost your mood and your creativity, makes it an easy choice. You'll feel a sense of pride when you complete your workout, which leads to a greater sense of confidence throughout your day.

Focusing on everything left on your to-do list at night and obsessing over what you didn't do. Instead, try creating what I call a "celebration list" where you acknowledge all of your daily accomplishments (even things that weren't originally on your to-do list). Celebration lists have become one of my favorite success rituals. They help build momentum when you see how much you actually got done. Momentum breeds confidence, and confidence makes you unstoppable.

look at your habitual daily actions and ask yourself if you are doing things that bring you closer to a place of self-confidence and feeling your absolute best. And if you're not, find the courage to eliminate those habits now.

HABIT AUDIT

What are some habits you'd like to eliminate?

_____

_____

_____

_____

_____

How would your life change if you gave these habits up?

_____

_____

_____

_____

What new habits can you introduce that help you build your confidence?

_____

_____

_____

_____

_____

POWER MANTRA

I am no longer available for disempowering beliefs,
toxic people, or anything that does not
support my highest self.

CHAPTER SEVEN

Success Is a State of Being

When I talk to women about success, one resounding feeling rings true for nearly all of them: They do not feel that they are successful as they should be.

Most of us learned from a young age to equate success with money and power. We put high-powered CEOs, rich entrepreneurs, and celebrities on pedestals, assuming that because they are "successful," they have it all. We click through their Instagram feeds in awe, we binge-watch their reality television shows, and we spend our hard-earned money to see them speak and perform. But do we ever wonder if those successful people are living life on their own terms? Do we ever wonder if they are being true to themselves? Do we ever wonder if they are actually happy?

Our culture has the notion of success backward. We've been taught to chase things outside ourselves, like executive titles, expensive cars, money, and fame, because we are taught that those things will prove us successful. We strive to be successful because we assume that success will bring us happiness. We spend our entire lives accumulating material things, working for six-figure salaries, and comparing our lives and our careers to everyone around us, and we wonder why we end up feeling unfulfilled, insecure, and exhausted.

One of my readers recently told me that she had finally achieved her lifelong dream of working as a hairstylist at New York Fashion Week. This dream was on every vision board she created and at the top of her career bucket list. She spent thousands of dollars on continuing education and worked for free on countless photo shoots and smaller runway events for exposure so that one day, she'd have the opportunity to travel to New York and work on one of those infamous shows. And finally, it happened. And she returned from Fashion Week completely underwhelmed. She had built the experience up so much in her mind, imagining that it would be inspiring and thrilling and ultimately make her feel successful—and it didn't. She told me that she felt like she had spent the last five years of her career working toward this one big moment, and now she felt disappointed and stuck with no direction.

My reader's disappointment was a beautiful lesson that success does not exist outside ourselves. How fortunate she was to learn this firsthand and be able to elevate her thinking! No career "win," accomplished goal, or experience will ever make us happy. We all get caught up in small thinking that goes something like this: *If I get to work at New York Fashion Week, I'll finally have made it!* or *If I get to take a vacation to Paris, I'll be so happy!* Of course we should strive for things. Of course we should desire things! But it is so important to release your expectations about these experiences and know that peace and joy and success *already* exist within us. It's our decision whether we want to tap into it. When we operate from a place of power, we understand that no one career opportunity, realized dream, or experience can bring us a sense of success. Success exists inside us. Success is a state of being. If we believe we are successful, we are. And that's all there is to it.

While researching for this book, I began sourcing articles and statistics on this very topic. Do you know that "How to be a successful woman in life" is one of the most popular Google searches? It broke my heart to see that, because it confirms that as women, for the most part, we still do not feel like we are measuring up. It confirms that we still think there's some sort of blueprint that we must follow if we want to achieve success. It confirms that we are still not confident in who we are. And we still don't think who we are is enough.

According to a survey done by *Glamour* magazine, 64 percent of women say they feel pressure to "make something of themselves," and 55 percent of women believe that being successful is "very stressful" or "high pressure." But the most fascinating piece in this research is that all of the two thousand women surveyed, when asked how they define success, used the same word: *happy*. When I survey my own audience on their idea of success, I see a similar story unfolding. They describe success in two parts: the first being the external things—money, accolades, rankings, and titles. And the second and often last-mentioned piece of success is happiness. "I just want to be happy" is typically the final wish on their laundry list of peripheral goals.

This means we are craving something deeper than fancy titles and big salaries. We believe success is something tangible to acquire, but deep down, we want more. We want to contribute to the world in a way that matters. We want to feel fulfilled, valued, and loved. We want to live our lives on our own terms, and although the pressure to be successful is undeniable, at the end of the day, we just want to—*be*.

BURN THE RULE BOOK: THERE IS NO FORMULA FOR SUCCESS

When I launched my life coaching practice, I remember looking around in my industry for inspiration. Because I was completely new to the field, I assumed I'd be able to find mentors and other coaches online to light me up and make me feel like everything was possible. I meticulously studied their websites, signed up for their email lists, and tuned into their webinars, hoping to discover some kind of rule book for "making it." I never did. Sure, I discovered some women who were doing cool things, but looking around confused me even more. I was inspired by certain aspects of their businesses but drained by others. It became all too overwhelming, and I quickly realized I had to look within myself to remember who I was, and ultimately build my confidence so I could put myself out there and produce work in my own style—work that I believed in; work that hadn't been done before. At least not in the way I could do it.

Not having a blueprint made me realize that achieving success was going to be an inside job. It was going to have to happen in a way that felt good for me, and I was the only one who could decide if I felt like a success. I had no idea how my potential clients would receive me. Would they take me seriously? Would they understand me? Would they connect with me?

The good news? Some did. The bad news? Some didn't. And that is one of the biggest lessons when it comes to building your self-worth: Not everyone is going to like you. And you've got to find a way to be okay with that. Not everyone is going to get what you're doing. And that's okay—in fact, that's a good sign. If every single person loves you, chances are you're not being true to yourself. If every single person loves you, you're most likely holding back the most colorful parts of yourself because you're worried about being rejected. But confident women don't live in a grayscale world. Confident women live in Technicolor; we live out loud; and we live with the knowledge that we won't be everyone's glass of champagne—and we don't need to be.

Here's a new idea: What if instead of chasing empty goals, we focused on being our truest selves? Because after all, isn't that when real success comes? What if we stripped away all the things we were taught about what makes a successful woman and thought about what actually matters to us? The ability to celebrate your authentic self is one of the best skills you will ever acquire. Each of us has different values. What's important to me may not be important to you. We all have different passions. What drives me may not do it for you. That's what makes this such a wonderful and interesting world. Can you imagine what it would be like if we all followed the exact same formula?

Spoiler alert: The formulas don't work. And if anyone tries to sell you one, run. It's impossible to duplicate someone else's success, because you are not that person. And you wouldn't want to be! Trying to do what someone else does is a fruitless effort, and the energy spent attempting that path could be energy spent discovering your own brilliance. Once you learn to embrace every single aspect of yourself—which is what I hope you've been able to do throughout this book—you realize just how special it is to get to be *you*. Never forget that you have something undeniably valuable and beautiful to contribute. *You already have everything you need.* Nothing outside yourself will make you a better woman: not money, not celebrity, not a ranking in your company, not a Chanel bag. You are already enough because you are you.

Let's take a few moments to dig into what makes you unique: What are some of your attributes that you're proud of?

_____

_____

_____

_____

_____

How do these attributes help you stand out?

_____

_____

_____

_____

_____

How can you celebrate these attributes more often?

_____

_____

_____

_____

MAKE ART, NOT GOALS

Have you ever looked at your notebook or vision board and felt completely misaligned with the goals you set for yourself? Have you ever stopped in the middle of your workday and felt totally disconnected from what you were doing?

I sure have, and it happened enough that I knew I had to totally change my relationship with goal setting. This may sound strange to you, but these days, I don't set goals. I know, it's confusing. How can someone who has written six (nearly seven!) books not set goals? Allow me to explain what I mean. I am not the kind of woman to say something like "I want to make a million dollars this year" or "I need to write fifteen thousand words this month." I've tried that approach, and it left me feeling resentful and rebellious. It also made me feel like a big fat failure because most of the time, I never met those goals, and I beat myself up for it time and time again. These days, I make my overall well-being a priority and get myself into a high vibration and *then* produce work out of that space. From that space come books, blog posts, podcasts, and more. From that space comes my best work, because I'm creating it from my best self. And the most interesting part of all of it? It doesn't even feel like work. When I create things from a high vibe, it feels as though my work is my art: a beautiful and true self-expression that I get to share with the world every day.

I recognize that this concept may flip everything you've ever learned about personal and professional development on its head. I recognize that my approach to success may raise some questions. How does one stay focused if there isn't a twenty-seven-page document detailing next steps? How does one remain committed to her work if there are no monthly targets? I want to make something clear: Altering your approach to goal setting is not about being lazy or unorganized. It's quite the opposite. I believe this approach actually helps you produce better work and do it more efficiently; it helps you produce the kind of work that feels aligned with your core desires. It helps you figure out what makes you happy, where you shine, and what feels right on a soul level. Quality over quantity, and the ability to trust your intuition, are key factors in defining success as your newly empowered self.

I started a podcast in early 2017 because I was looking for a way to connect with my readers that stretched beyond my books and social media. I wanted to provide valuable content and actionable tools to my audience on a weekly basis, and a podcast sounded like a great way to do that. Prior to launching, I didn't study any other podcasters in my industry. I didn't even know my phone had a podcast app! The only experience I had with podcasts was being a guest on someone else's. I had done radio for years, but this was new territory for me. Rather than obsessively researching what everyone else in the industry was doing and ultimately defining my idea of success based on what was already out there, I went into the project with blinders on. I focused on self-love and self-care, and I dug deep to figure out what I wanted to teach. I immersed myself in recording my shows and sharing them with my audience. In fact, it wasn't until about five months in that I started subscribing to other podcasts and tuning into what was happening in the space. The result? A top-rated show with record numbers in just a few short months.

I believe that if had I spent months researching other podcasts and setting a bar for myself based on what had been done before, I would have set myself up for failure. I would have gotten trapped in a cycle of comparison, self-doubt, and insecurity. My voice would have been drowned out by others, and my creative juices would have run dry. That's what happens when we search for the answers outside ourselves: We forget just how much we already have access to inside.

I used to make vision boards religiously. The idea of a vision board is to keep your goals in front of you so you are reminded of what you want and consciously work toward making it happen. Every January, I created a board overflowing with images, many of them completely superfluous, that represented my goals. Magazine cutouts of words like *fame* and pictures of talk show sets were plastered all over my board, which I always had professionally framed. I even included a photo of Khloe Kardashian once, in the hopes that she would somehow discover my books and hire me to be her personal life coach. Are you cringing? Because I sure am.

I believed these things would help me gain more success and ultimately make me happy. And it wasn't until one summer afternoon when I was rearranging my apartment that I realized just how wrong I'd had it. I can recall looking at that particular vision board with Khloe's face on it, thinking, *What the hell is this? This is not who I am. I don't even want these things anymore.* It was in that moment that I decided instead of vision boards, I was going to start making what I call happiness boards. I'm a creative, so I didn't want to give up the art of making something inspiring that I could hang in my apartment. But this time, I approached it completely differently. I decided to get a corkboard where I could pin images that simply made me happy. I chose a corkboard because I could swap in new things whenever I wanted. Because after all, I'm constantly finding new things that make me happy.

Whether it was a card from one of my readers, a photo of me and my friends celebrating something special, a magazine clipping from a piece of press I was featured in, or a quote I love, the point was to collect things that made me feel good. It was less about a collection of things to drive me toward some outside goal and more about reminding myself of everything I love. My new method of making happiness boards has had a direct impact on the way I feel every day, and I've turned so many women on to this strategy as well.

If you've been feeling disconnected from your work, I urge you to take some time to review your current projects. If you're an entrepreneur, are you enjoying the work you're doing? Do you still feel challenged? Do you feel you're truly living your purpose and reaching your potential? Or are you checking goals off a list because that's what others in your industry are doing?

If you're in a corporate job, it's okay to ask yourself if that job is still making you happy. Are you just going through the motions because you've got a "good deal"? I remember that back when I was working my full-time job and considering leaving to pursue my dreams, a lot of people told me I had a good deal. I had been there for eight years, I had an executive title, and I was making six figures. On the outside, I'm sure it did look like a good deal. But I had to be very careful to separate their idea of good from mine and understand that comfort does not equal success.

Regardless of your specific job title, I recommend spending some time alone, in meditation or journaling (or both), and being honest with yourself. Spend a few weeks really doubling down on your self-care and your wellness. Make sure you're getting regular exercise (or at least getting up from your desk and taking a long walk each day), as well as eating nutritious foods and getting good sleep. When you get into a space where you are operating at a high frequency, you're able to think more clearly. Are you making art? Or are you making goals?

WHAT'S CASH GOT TO DO WITH IT?

It can be tempting to equate success with money. After all, financial independence is very important. Who wants to depend on anyone else to pay their bills? Who wants to have to ask permission to buy themself something? Not I! Conversations about money fascinate me, because for me, money is simply an energy. It's not something to be obsessed with, and it's not something to be afraid of. Money brings freedom. It brings the means to create opportunities for ourselves and others. And we all need it to survive. But where do we draw the line between financial independence and blindly chasing big monetary goals because they sound good?

There's a big trend in the entrepreneur world to have a "million-dollar business." I never quite understood this fantasy. What does a million-dollar business even mean? Does that mean you have a million dollars in your business bank account? Does it mean you own a million dollars' worth of assets? Does it mean you generate a million dollars per year in revenue? Yet still, I see woman after woman setting "million-dollar goals" and posting quotes about million-dollar mind-sets all over Instagram. This isn't necessarily a bad thing, and I'm certainly not knocking what drives a person. But I urge people to ask themselves why they're driven by monetary goals. What's the motivator for racing toward one million dollars? Or one hundred thousand dollars? Is it the money you want, or the feeling of freedom? Because the two are very different.

The same can be argued in the corporate world, where we chase new jobs with bigger and bigger salaries, assuming that a larger yearly income will fill a void. And while I absolutely believe women should be paid well, we can't assume that with a bigger bank account comes happiness. We must ask ourselves other important questions: *Am I excited to get up each day and do what I'm about to do? Does my work fulfill me? Am I challenged intellectually and creatively?* I'm of the school of thought that when you do what you love, the money will come. I know this because I've experienced it firsthand. By my third year of full-time entrepreneurship, I had nearly tripled the corporate salary I was earning when I left MTV, and I hadn't even set out to do so. I focused on what I was passionate about, I worked hard, and it happened. And guess what? It's not the tripled salary that makes me happy. It's the feeling I get waking up every single day knowing I'm about to do something meaningful. It's the freedom to live a life I love.

Want to know something even more personal? For a while, I was earning my income solely through my book sales. Which meant I didn't have to do a whole lot of work day to day. I was bringing in a very healthy passive income each month, but I wasn't challenged. I hadn't done anything new in a while. I felt bored and uninspired. I had to find something in me to drive me beyond making money. The cash was there, so it would've been very easy to sit back and collect a royalty check and shop all day. And if I'm being honest, I did exactly that for a while. But I knew I couldn't sustain that kind of life because I thrive on new challenges. I live for the hustle. I get off on putting myself up to all sorts of new projects. I had to dig deep and light a fire under myself that was not inspired by a monetary goal, because I didn't need more money. And I learned more about self-discipline and motivation during that time than ever before.

I realize some of you may be reading this and thinking, *Sure, Cara, it's easy to say money doesn't matter when you have it!* I'm personally acquainted with the stress of being broke. I was raised by a single mother who worked two jobs and put herself through college at age forty to support my brother and me. My father did not contribute at all, so she was left to do it alone. And she did an *incredible* job. But I know what it's like to not have things. My mother tells us all the time about how when we were kids, she'd have to unscrew the same lightbulb and bring it from room to room because she couldn't afford to buy a new one until she got paid again.

Would it have been great to grow up in a huge house with a pool and a car and enough lightbulbs for every room? Absolutely! But I learned from a young age that money can't substitute for happiness, or emotional support, or creativity, or love. You've got to find those things within. And kudos to my mother, because although we may have been poor financially, we were so rich in every other way.

As I got older, my relationship with money had its ups and downs. I misused it for a long time. I've been knee deep in credit card debt, dodging calls from debt collectors because I couldn't even afford my minimum payment. I've tried to stretch $10 until payday. I've had to borrow money from my mom, at thirty years old. Those things left me feeling less than confident.

We all need a baseline of cash to allow us to live without struggle. But remember, according to all that research I mentioned earlier, women just want to be happy. So how exactly *does* money tie into happiness? And is there a dollar amount to satisfy that?

You'll find this interesting. According to a popular 2010 academic study by psychologist Daniel Kahneman and economist Angus Deaton, as people strive to reach $75,000 per year, their happiness does rise. But after that, happiness plateaus. Earning more money has no measurable effect on everyday happiness. Perhaps an indication that the happiness *is* in the hustle? That study, which analyzed more than 450,000 responses, indicates that beyond our basic living expenses, perhaps we should be chasing things other than cash to feel happier.

Of course, this study is an average example. Your financial needs may be completely different. Depending on the city you live in, and the size of your family and those dependent on you, you may require a different level of income to cover your expenses. But the main takeaway here is that just adding more and more money to your salary will most likely not change your day-to-day levels of happiness. So it's worth thinking about what other variables could define success for you.

I invite you to rewrite your definition of success:

_____

_____

_____

_____

_____

How would your life change if you lived by that new definition?

_____

_____

_____

_____

REJECTION IS REDIRECTION

When I was in the second grade, I declared to the world that I was going to be an author when I grew up. For a class project, I wrote a children's book called *The Cat Who Couldn't Fit In*, which I proudly assembled with felt and contact paper. I not only wrote the book, but I illustrated it and even included an About the Author paragraph on the back cover. I described, in detail, my future life as a writer who lived in Virginia on a farm filled with horses.

As I grew up, my dream of becoming a writer and author remained, but life took over, as it does, leading me down many different roads. By age twenty-eight, I wasn't pounding on my typewriter while my horses watched me through my Virginia farmhouse windows. Instead, I found myself working at MTV as a digital ad trafficker. If you don't know what that is, it's not important; it's about as mind-numbing as it sounds. I was making a good salary, I had health insurance, and I was completely miserable. Because everyone had always told me writers don't make money, I decided that, rather than try to switch careers, I'd start a blog on the side as a creative outlet. I still secretly clung to my dream of writing a book one day, but I focused on the blog first as a chance to explore my ideas and sharpen my skills.

My blog became my passion. I fell so in love with sharing my stories that I decided to start working on that book just a few months later. The experience of writing my first book was exhilarating. I poured every ounce of myself into the process, and when the time came to put together a proposal and find an agent, I was already imagining walking into my boss's office, slamming a copy of my book deal on his desk, and dancing out while waving my middle finger in the air. I could taste my publishing fantasy, and failure was not an option for me.

Until it was.

For nearly one year, I worked closely with my literary agent to perfect the proposal and shop it around to publishers. My first rejection rolled in right before Christmas. And then came another. And another. And another. I was ultimately rejected by nineteen publishers before deciding to part ways with my agent and retire my dream of traditional publishing. But I didn't retire my dream of being an author altogether. At that point, I could have let that failure define me, or I could let it redirect me. I chose redirection and self-published my first book, *Sparkle*, with the support of my blog readers, friends, and family behind me. I even threw myself a small book signing at my local bookstore. I was determined to turn my fantasy into reality, even if the path looked a little different.

Sparkle rose to the top of the Amazon charts as soon as it was released. I reached out to blogs and online magazines and pitched myself to gain press for the book. I passed out copies at networking events. I asked my readers to post photos of themselves with the book, and I shared them all over my social media. I decided to self-publish my next book the following year, and then the next, and in 2015, I self-published my fourth book, *Girl Code*, the book that put me on the map and ultimately changed my life.

Call it divine timing, call it hard work finally paying off, but *Girl Code* opened me up to opportunities I didn't even know were possible. Not only did I consistently sell enough copies that writing became my full-time job and my main source of income (and who said writers don't make money!?), but I also had the chance to connect with women from around the world who were finding the book and falling in love with it. One of my proudest moments was traveling to Tokyo and meeting a group of women who were using *Girl Code* to learn English while simultaneously becoming empowered in their lives and careers.

And one of the biggest highlights of my experience with self-publishing? The success of *Girl Code* impressed the folks at Portfolio Books enough to offer me a book deal. As Steve Jobs said, you can't always connect the dots looking forward, but you can connect them looking back. I now know that my initial rejection was a form of protection. My journey was meant to unfold the way it did. I wasn't meant to get a book deal when I was twenty-eight years old. And in retrospect, I'm so glad I didn't. I had the opportunity to evolve as a woman, to prove to myself that I could be successful on my own terms, and to realize that as amazing as it is to have a publisher, it's not necessary. I removed my co-dependency from that dream, and I can now enjoy it for everything it is. And let me tell you, it's fucking fantastic to experience success as a strong, confident, independent woman.

Life changes when we begin to view failure as an experience rather than the end point. When we view rejection as redirection. Just because something doesn't go as planned does not mean you've failed. Don't view a plot twist as a reason to close the book on your dreams. Successful women know that the more times they fail, the stronger, wiser, and more seasoned they become. This may sound totally crazy, but sometimes I ask the universe to let me fail. When things feel too easy, I invite a challenge into my life because I believe that challenges are where our biggest lessons live. Failure gives me an opportunity to become more self-aware; it gives me something to teach, and many times, my failures lead me to my greatest successes.

If you're terrified of failure, you should know that failure is not only normal, it's also a learning experience necessary to eventual success. You'd be surprised at how intimate some the most famous, revered women in history had to become with failure before they experienced success. Trust me, you'll want to be in their company.

Four Favorite Women Who Owned Their Failures

Marilyn Monroe. Although she was one of the world's most beloved, beautiful women, Marilyn Monroe experienced her fair share of failure throughout her career. Marilyn wanted nothing more than to be taken seriously as an actress, but was dropped by 20th Century Fox because they reportedly felt she lacked talent. And do you know what Ms. Monroe did? She started her very own production company, Marilyn Monroe Productions, and created the kind of roles for herself that she had once dreamed of landing through Fox. She leveraged her rejection and turned it into redirection. Sound familiar? She carved her own path, became her own advocate, worked hard, and soon enough, she proved herself. Marilyn wound up negotiating a brand-new seven-year contract with Fox that gave her more money and more control, and ultimately led her to command the industry that once rejected her.

Oprah Winfrey. There aren't enough words in the English language to describe my admiration for Oprah. And as adored as she is by millions of people, Oprah wasn't quite as respected early on in her career. She was demoted at one of her first jobs on television after being told she wasn't the right fit for the evening news. Devastated but still determined, Oprah took a shot at a new position with the company, co-hosting a daytime talk show called *People Are Talking*. Little did she know that experience would set her on a trajectory that would change not only her own life, but the world. Oprah believed in herself and kept trying new things, proving to us that sometimes unexpected failures are the very things that shape us into who we are.

Madonna. It's hard to fathom that someone as insanely talented, unapologetic, and badass as Madonna would ever be touched by rejection. Yet after researching her essays, interviews, and documentaries, I learned that she had been rattled badly, and not for the reasons you might assume. While she was used to public scrutiny surrounding her provocative career moments, she wasn't prepared for the backlash she'd receive after deciding to adopt her children from Africa. Challenged by the Supreme Court, accused of kidnapping, child trafficking, and bribery, Madonna faced a firestorm for simply trying to save her children's lives. She describes it as one of the lowest points of her life but worth every second. A quote from the 2013 essay she wrote for *Harper's Bazaar* reads, "If you aren't willing to fight for what you believe in, then don't even enter the ring." Madonna could have given up her fight and moved on. But she refused to take no for an answer.

Arianna Huffington. We know her as a media mogul, bestselling author, and all-around powerhouse, but while her first book was a huge success, did you know that Arianna Huffington's second book was rejected by thirty-six publishers? I love this story, obviously, because as an author it reminds me that we must keep innovating, keep fighting for our work, and never get too comfortable. Arianna has said, "You can recognize very often that out of these projects that may not have succeeded themselves that other successes are built." She's now the author of thirteen books and continues to be a trusted authority on women in the workplace.

Think about a time in your life when you failed.

_____

_____

_____

_____

_____

What did that failure teach you?

_____

_____

_____

_____

_____

How can you allow that failure to redirect you?

_____

_____

_____

_____

_____

POWER MANTRA

Success does not exist outside myself.
It is my natural state of being.

CHAPTER EIGHT

Magic, the Ego, and Your Fantasy World

Keep some room in your heart for
the unimaginable.

—MARY OLIVER

U p to this point, we've laid down some laws of logic, transformational tools, and motivational methods for building your confidence. And while I love a good set of steps, I also love a little magic. Those soulful feelings, those unexplainable synchronicities, and those mystical moments that are hard to define are what make life exciting. I haven't met one woman who has evolved into her most beautiful and brilliant self who relied purely on rational behavior. There's a certain level of spirituality and faith—and I'm not talking about religion—that sprinkles that extra dose of inspiration into our journey. So cast aside your tool kit and grab your magical wand. We're going in, baby.

EVERYTHING IS ENERGY

Have you ever gone to a concert and as soon as the lights went down and the crowd roared and your favorite artist took the stage, you felt an instant surge of happiness? Have you ever felt totally exhausted and not in the mood to exercise, but the moment you walked into your fitness class and heard the music blasting and saw everyone in their workout clothes you felt ready? Alternatively, have you ever walked into a room and felt a bad vibe or a dark cloud as soon as you entered? Those physical and emotional shifts you feel are not coincidence—they are energy. And the kind of energy you tap into will either change your life or suck it right out of you.

You might have heard the term *high vibration* before. Being in a high vibration typically means experiencing feelings of happiness, positivity, optimism, and love. It's the feeling you have when you're aligned with what you truly desire, when you're fully expressing yourself and genuinely feeling good. On the flip side, if you're in a low vibration, you're most likely feeling emotionally drained, physically exhausted, hopeless, stuck, frustrated, jealous, or angry. Not a good place to be, especially when you're taking control of your life and cultivating your confidence. What we focus on expands, so if we're obsessing over everything that's going wrong in our lives, we're going to keep getting more of that.

I can vividly recall working in my corporate job and having to attend weekly meetings with everyone in my department. The meetings were held on Monday mornings, in a large conference room lit up by fluorescent bulbs and packed with gray folding chairs. Every Monday at nine A.M., employees would pile into the room like sardines to be prepped for the week ahead. I remember looking around that room at everyone's faces and feeling so depressed. No one looked excited or energized; in fact, they all looked completely fucking miserable. The negative energy was palpable, so bad that after the meetings I'd have to go outside to take a few deep breaths and shake off those bad vibes that I felt penetrating my mind and my body. At the time, I knew that my job—and these meetings—were no good for me. But now when I look back at photos of myself throughout those years, I can see the sadness in my eyes. I looked pale and unhealthy. I looked lifeless.

Leaving that job and moving into a career that I'm deeply passionate about was a game changer for me. Of course, there are still struggles and I'm still faced with anxiety and challenging days, but I removed a massive energy block—the experience of working in an environment that stifled my creativity, held me back from my biggest dreams, and bored me to tears. Now, despite the hard times, I am still brimming with positive energy because I am making a confident choice every single day to live a life I'm proud of. I'm making a confident choice every day to pursue my desires, exist in a high vibration, and actively create the world I want to live in.

But that took time. What if you can't just run away from that job or that relationship or *that thing* that is draining your energy? Lord knows it took me years to plan my escape from corporate America, and I had to figure out how to get through the days where I was hanging on by a thread and absorbing all the crap around me. I want you to understand that both energies—high vibrations and low vibrations—are within our control. People get stuck in a negative place just because they wake up in a bad mood, or they find themselves in a soul-sucking job and they accept that energetic state. They assume that vibration has power over them, and they give up before they even start trying to shift it. There is no doubt that our circumstances and environment can and will affect our energy. But it's totally possible to make internal changes that help you feel better and ultimately change the trajectory of your life. Because it all begins there.

Getting into a high vibration is the fastest way to supercharge your soul and start taking massive, inspired action to create your ideal world. The bad news? Changing your situation takes time and patience. The great news? Great energy all begins with your thoughts, and you can redirect those at any time. There is no excuse to fill your mind with negativity. In this chapter, I'm going to share a few of my tried-and-true techniques for instantly transforming your energy into a space of possibility and positivity, and experiencing the magic that makes life worth living.

What does your current energetic state feel like?

_____

_____

_____

_____

_____

Can you recall a time in your life when you felt like you were in a high vibration?

_____

_____

_____

_____

_____

What steps can you take to shift into a high vibration right now?

_____

_____

_____

_____

CHANNELING YOUR INNER MUSE

I restore myself when I'm alone.
—MARILYN MONROE

A powerful woman lives inside each one of us. She's you minus the limiting beliefs we talked about in Chapter One. She's you minus the insecurity and the self-doubt. She's you minus the

OMG what will they say about me? She's you minus the anxiety of beginning something new. She's you minus the constant loop of negative self-talk and disempowering beliefs. She's you minus the fear of the rug getting pulled out from under you. She's you minus the bullshit, and she is the woman who will save your life.

Here's what I wish I could have told myself in the years before I left MTV, when I often fell victim to these kinds of thoughts. I wish I had known that I didn't need to shrink myself just because those around me didn't understand me. I wish I had spent more time getting to know *my* inner muse and had the guts to let her play a little—even if only in my cubicle at first. I wish I had realized that the sooner I channeled her, the sooner I would have built up the courage to quit that job and live life on my own terms. I probably would have dyed my hair pink sooner, told more people about my creative work, and spent less time fretting about the future and more time being in the present moment.

If you're finding yourself stuck in a place where you feel out of whack with who you truly are deep down and what circumstance you're in—whether that be an unfulfilling job, a crappy relationship, or an unhealthy body—try doing small things to get in touch with yourself. Maybe it's wearing an outfit you're dying to wear, and simply saying "fuck it" when the self-doubt creeps in. Maybe it's dyeing the ends of your hair purple (you'll have a full head in no time). Maybe it's creating a morning mantra to help guide you through your day fearlessly. All of those things will empower you with the tools to remember that you're in control of your life, and despite your situation, you're actively moving toward the place you want to be.

Whenever I embark on a new project, whether it's writing a new book, evolving my personal style, or taking on a new hobby, I'm always seeking inspiration. I used to make the mistake of thinking that inspiration was only going to be found outside me. Of course, many of us (myself included) are inspired by art, music, travel, or other people who are doing amazing things, but I eventually realized that the deepest and truest inspiration happens inside. Even the word *inspiration* has the word *in* at the beginning of it. Use that as a reminder that you have everything you need. And everything you need can be accessed through your inner muse.

The concept of the muse dates back to ancient times. Both Greek and Roman poets believed that all creative work was inspired by a muse, a goddesslike being who was the daughter of Zeus and Mnemosyne, the goddess of memory. According to this myth, the muse would descend upon the poet as a sort of creative companion, downloading ideas and words and, ultimately, the art that the poet would create in the form of writing, or "musings." The poet felt that he was simply a conduit for the muse's message, and he was not responsible for what came from this divine inspiration. He was, however, incredibly grateful, because a muse could strike without warning, and there was no promise of her return.

When you're feeling uncertain, drained, or insecure, just remember that you are your own damn muse.

Since the Greeks and Romans developed the concept of the muse, we've learned so much more about the psychology of the mind and how our brains function. We now know that we all exist on two planes of consciousness: the ego and the id. The ego is our rational mind. It makes plans, sets goals, and acts in a rather logical manner. The id is our subconscious mind, filled with feelings, memories, and more primal or instinctual thought processes. We can now connect the id with our inner muse and realize that often that creative spark, or "aha" moment, is unearthed through our subconscious mind—the place where our inner muse lives.

Unlike the ancient poets, we now understand that we can channel our inner muse willingly. When you're in a high vibration, feeling all sorts of positive vibes flowing through you, it's easier to connect with your inner muse. It's almost as if she's bubbled up to the surface, constantly feeding you ideas and inspiration. She's so close you can almost feel her presence as she floats around your mental atmosphere, jolting you with epiphanies and lightbulb moments. She is confident, creative, and free of the rational chains that often shackle us. Whether she's helping you become more self-aware and see things in a new light, giving you new business ideas, or providing the inspiration to write your new book or the courage to dye your hair pink, there's no doubt that your inner muse is a direct reflection of your energetic state. She is your deepest, truest, best self coming forward.

But don't be freaked out if you have a hard time finding her. The best parts of ourselves often take time to access, for many different reasons. Remember those limiting beliefs we talked about

You can reconnect with your inner muse (or meet her for the first time ever) by using these strategies:

Meditate. Find a quiet space where you can dedicate at least fifteen minutes to sit in meditation. Set a clear intention to connect with your muse. As you breathe in, welcome her. As you exhale, release the ego-driven thoughts of control or self-criticism. Remember, your muse is playful, free-spirited, and filled with creativity. She needs room to defy logic and express herself without bounds.

Make a playlist. Music is a powerful escape and a chance to set the tone (pun totally intended) to connect with your muse. Choose songs that put you in the zone, make you feel empowered, and help bring your muse to the surface. If your muse is sassy and bold, perhaps listening to a Madonna album will evoke her. If your muse is sensitive and artful, perhaps a jazz playlist is what you need.

Dress the part. One of my favorite things about our inner muse is her sense of boldness. No matter your personal style, you must know that your muse breaks all the rules in life and in fashion. My muse loves the color pink, isn't afraid to rock a faux fur jacket, and thrives on individuality. Let's put it this way: Your muse probably isn't wearing beige slacks. Have fun experimenting with your wardrobe when channeling inspiration. And if you feel silly, blame it on her.

Ask yourself: What Would My Muse Do? (WWMMD?) Once you get to know this fierce, fiery woman inside

> you, start leaning on her for advice. Nervous about ask-
> ing for a raise at work? Scared to wear that new bold lip
> color? Afraid to tell your lover you aren't satisfied in the
> bedroom? Ask yourself, *What would my inner muse do?*
> And act accordingly.

in the first chapter? They can do a number on you, making it more challenging to invite your inner muse to the table. If you find yourself in a regular state of high anxiety, it can also be hard to find her because you're clouded with nervous thoughts and negative chatter in your mind. My muse was lost for a good seven years during one of my long-term relationships. Because of how toxic things were, I buried her without even realizing I had dug her grave. I was so focused on making my then-boyfriend happy and changing myself in the hope that he would accept me that the best part of me seemed gone forever. The best part of that breakup? Getting to know her again. And man, was she happy to be back.

And please remember this: Channeling your inner muse is meant to be fun! She's all about unapologetic confidence and living beyond fear. Commit to her way of thinking and set yourself free.

When I wrote my book of poetry called *Stripped* in 2016, I relied heavily on my inner muse to guide me throughout the process. I am not a poet, I did not study poetry, and I had no idea if the book was going to work. I did, however, feel completely compelled to write it, and during the writing process, the words flowed from me like a rushing waterfall. I was completely plugged in to my muse, embodying her in every way. Channeling her helped me defy the imposter syndrome that could have easily crept in. I stayed focused on the inspiration flowing from me. I was so connected that much of that time felt like a blur, something almost beyond my control. I surrendered to her and let my creativity take the wheel. And the result was a beautiful book that was received by my readers more positively than I could have ever imagined.

When you live and work from that inner space, you commit to your authenticity. Your muse isn't faking it; she's as real as they come. And people can sense it. Have you ever admired a woman who effortlessly and unapologetically does her own thing? She's not worried about what everyone else is doing. She is connected to her muse, and that's all the inspiration she needs.

TRUST YOUR GUT—
THAT BITCH KNOWS WHAT'S UP

We can't talk about your inner muse without talking about intuition. Do you know how to instantly become consumed with self-doubt? By asking everyone around you for permission. Have you ever asked someone for their opinion, only to still feel unsure, and then ask another person, and another? Soon enough, you've polled basically everyone you know, and although you have more "answers" than ever, you're more confused and unsure of yourself than when you began. Empowered women don't poll. Empowered women may request feedback from a small circle of trusted confidants, or they may not request feedback at all. But one thing is certain: They rely heavily on their intuition.

Over the years, I have become intimate with my own intuition. I instinctively know when a business opportunity is not right for me or when I don't trust someone. I have a sharp sense of when I should move forward with an idea or when I should back away from it. This has taken years of practice: paying attention to that voice in the back of my head, paying attention to my patterns and what works for me, paying attention to how I *feel* in a certain situation. Sometimes only I can see a vision for myself, and my gut tells me I need to pursue it. If I waited for everyone around me to get on board, there's a strong chance I could be waiting forever.

In order to get comfortable trusting this superpower we all have access to, start practicing the gut check. Ask yourself, *What is my intuition telling me about this situation?* First, observe your feelings without judgment. Then try acting on that intuitive sense. If you're nervous about doing this with major decisions, start small and build up over time as you learn to trust yourself.

The power of intuition has been linked to success and supported by entrepreneurs like Steve Jobs, who said, "Intuition is a very powerful thing, more powerful than intellect, in my opinion. That's had a big impact on my work." Oprah also swears by listening to her gut. "Learning to trust your instincts, using your intuitive sense of what's best for you, is paramount for any lasting success. I've trusted the still, small voice of intuition my entire life. And the only time I've made mistakes is when I didn't listen," she wrote in an article on her website. "When you don't know what to do, do nothing. Get quiet so you can hear the still, small voice—your inner GPS guiding you to true North."

WHY YOU SHOULD LIVE IN A FANTASY WORLD

When I was seventeen, I started a music magazine out of my bedroom with my good friend Jen. My dream was to be a music journalist, and I couldn't wait until after college to get a job in the industry, so I created one. Patience was never my thing and I knew the power of choosing yourself early on. Jen and I carefully planned each issue, listing out all the albums we wanted to review and the bands we wanted to feature. We even included poetry and quotes we collected from our friends and favorite artists. We knew we had to be taken seriously to gain press passes to concerts and music festivals, so we gave ourselves titles and made our own letterhead on our clunky desktop computers. I collected the names and addresses of record labels from the backs of my CDs and called them to arrange our interviews.

"Hello, this is Cara Alwill, editor in chief of *Honeyspider Magazine*," I'd proudly tell the receptionist, praying she'd patch me through to the public relations department so I could make my pitch. When I couldn't get through on the phone, I'd mail a letter in the hopes that someone—anyone—would get back to me and help me turn my dreams into a reality. And guess what? Most of them did.

Before graduating high school, I had already interviewed bands like Blink 182 and Metallica. I was busy scoring VIP passes to the Warped Tour while my classmates were busy scoring pot. I was as serious as ever about becoming a music journalist, and nothing was going to get in my way. While my friends were cutting class to smoke up behind the school, I was cutting class and getting on the subway to go intern at TVT Records for no money and no school credit. All I wanted was to be around the music industry and the people who worked in it—I didn't care about getting paid. Every afternoon, I'd walk up to that big brick-orange building on East 4th Street and find my way to the main conference room, where my boss would let me preview new albums while assembling press kits. I was in heaven.

Those days of being a "girl boss" before the term *girl boss* actually existed shaped me in a big way. I learned early on that I was the master of my destiny, and I had the ability to create the kind of world I wanted to live in. I made no money doing my zine or being an intern, but I didn't care. One day, while I was visiting my mom at work, her boss asked me how much the record label was paying me. "I'm not in it for the money" was my reply, and my mom and her boss laughed and laughed. They couldn't grasp how I could be so passionate about a job that didn't pay me. Sure, it would've been nice to get a paycheck each week, but that wasn't happening, and I wasn't letting that stand in the way of my ultimate goal. While most people were telling me to be "more realistic" about my dreams, I was busy figuring out who I could

So how does one bring those fantasies to fruition? Because after all, we want to bridge the gap between fantasy and reality and live out those dreams in real life, right? I've developed a few core strategies that I turn to when I want to begin birthing a big dream.

Fight for your write! If you haven't already purchased a dedicated journal to have with you as you go through this book, the time is now. Writing down what you want is your biggest ally in attaining happiness, confidence, and success. I'm talking about writing—not typing. We spend our lives on our phones and our computers, so the art of writing your dreams by hand automatically becomes a special experience. And there's science to back this claim up. In 2014, the Association of Psychological Science reported that students who physically took notes received a memory boost—particularly when compared to those who took notes via a laptop. Use a pretty journal and place it somewhere safe in your home or your office. Every time you write, make it a ritual. Light candles, pour a glass of wine or a cup of tea, and commit to the experience.

Establish a dream team. Whether it's your spouse, your closest friends, or like-minded women you meet in a Facebook group, assemble a dream team of people you can share your fantasy with. When you're going big, there's a chance you'll be faced with those who tell you it can't be done, simply because they don't have the capacity to think the way you do. By reserving your fantasies for the ones who "get it," you'll be sure to receive the support you need in cooking up those big ideas.

Rewrite your beliefs about yourself. Rewrite your current belief set in the form of affirmations. For example, if your fantasy involves bringing more wealth and abundance into your life, and you're used to being afraid of money and feeling like there's never enough, you'll need to change your beliefs about wealth. Your new affirmation could read something like this: "I am no longer available for feelings of lack. I know my worth, and I'm ready for abundance in all areas of my life."

Create a game plan. Once you're clear on what your dreams are, it's time to start taking inspired action. One of my biggest fantasies is to one day own the eighties dance club I go to every weekend. In order to take this from a fantasy to a reality, I need to start making moves to see it come to fruition. I am a big believer in creating small, actionable steps as you build up to your big huge dream. So one of my goals may be learning more about the business and talking to the manager to understand how the club works. I may want to meet the patrons and find out what their needs are. Later on down the line, my goal may be setting up a meeting with the current owners to see if they're interested in ever selling the place. When you break things down into bite-sized chunks, your big-picture fantasy suddenly starts to seem attainable. And that's where the momentum begins. And momentum builds confidence. And confidence fuels you to ultimately change your life.

connect with to help me make them happen. I didn't take *no* for an answer, and I built my own doors when the ones I tried to open were slammed in my face.

I've carried that entrepreneurial spirit with me throughout the years, and it's now my mission to help every woman realize that she is the boss of her own life—even if she doesn't own her own business. Every woman has the ability to step into her power and re-create her reality, no matter how out of reach it may feel. And the first step is developing a healthy relationship with fantasizing. Have you ever caught yourself staring off into space, dreaming up a scenario that you know would make you happy? Or falling asleep at night, imagining something playing out in your mind in the most favorable way possible? Those brief moments where we catch ourselves in a daydream are the seeds of true change. Those are the moments we must seize, nurture, and expand upon. As Gloria Steinem says, "Dreaming, after all, is a form of planning."

Everyone's reality is completely different. What's true for me may not be true for you. It's important to identify the fantasy that feels good to you. This is the time to use your imagination and to visualize without limits. This is the time to cast aside the fear, the doubt, and the worry about what's "right" or "wrong." This is the time to let magic show up and take the wheel.

What does your fantasy world look like?

_____

_____

_____

_____

_____

Do you believe this fantasy can come true?

_____

_____

_____

_____

If not, how can you start to believe it?

_____

_____

_____

_____

_____

What steps can you take right now to make your fantasy world possible?

_____

_____

_____

_____

_____

POWER MANTRA

My natural energetic state is one of love, joy, and possibility. I attract everything I desire effortlessly and without struggle.

In Conclusion

hope if you take one thing away from this book, it's that confidence is accessible to you at any time you wish to find it. Confidence is a gift you can give yourself in every moment. It is your ally, your truest, most natural state. Building your confidence is less about learning and more about unlearning all the things we thought we knew about ourselves.

You have everything you need within you to thrive. You are not broken; you are actually so whole that it terrifies the world that tries to keep you small.

I hope you know that your past does not define you. It never did, and it never will. Your story can be rewritten at any time, and self-reinvention is one of the most exhilarating experiences ever, if you let it be.

I hope this book has helped you realize that you *do* own the place. You always have. And I hope you realize that "the place" is actually yourself. You may find yourself lost and unlost inside your own bones from time to time, but you can always come home. She'll be waiting for you. Always.

WITH LOVE,
CARA

ACKNOWLEDGMENTS

To my mother, for always believing in me, even when you were terrified of my next move (and rightfully so!): I would be lost without you. To my darling husband, who has been my biggest fan and support system from day one: I love you. To my brother, for always being my sounding board and my dancing partner. To my dearest friends, who listen to my wild ideas, throw me business baby showers, laugh with me, and keep my secrets. To my brilliant editor, Leah, for seeing my potential, guiding me through one of the most challenging projects of my life, and making my biggest dream come true. To the entire team at Portfolio Books for making this book possible and letting me be me. And lastly, to my dedicated readers, podcast listeners, and Slay Babies: You are the reason I wake up every single day and get to do what I do. Thank you for your undying support and your endless love.

NOTES

CHAPTER ONE: Who Do You Think You Are?

12 men had higher self-esteem: Wiebke Bleidorn, "Age and Gender Differences in Self-Esteem—A Cross-Cultural Window," *Journal of Personality and Social Psychology* 11, no. 3 (2016).

13 seven in ten girls believe that they: "Real Girls, Real Pressure: National Report on the State of Self-Esteem," Dove Self-Esteem Fund, 2013, http://www.heartofleadership.org/statistics.

13 "immense pressure to look a certain way": Brent Donnellan, "Low Self-Esteem Is Related to Aggression, Anti-Social Behavior, and Delinquency," *Psychological Science* 16, no. 4 (2004).

13 girls say they feel pressured: "The Supergirl Dilemma: Girls Grapple with the Mounting Pressure of Expectations," Girls, Inc., 2006, http://www.girlsincyork.org/campaigns/supergirl-dilemma.

15 According to the Anxiety: Anxiety and Depression Association of America, https://adaa.org/living-with-anxiety/women/facts#, accessed March 29, 2018.

22 authenticity is a daily practice: Brené Brown, "Cultivating Authenticity—Letting Go of What Other People Think," The Value of Sparrows, 2014, https://thevalueofsparrows.com/2014/07/07/authenticity-cultivating -authenticity-letting-go-of-what-people-think-by-brene-brown.

NOTES

CHAPTER TWO: What We Talk About When We Talk About Beauty

32 Dr. Carmen Lefevre weighed in: Carmen Lefevre, quoted in Daniela Morosini, "So Much of Beauty Is Fake News, So Why Are We Still Sucked In?" *Refinery29*, September 2, 2017, http://www.refinery29.com/2017/08/170671/fake-instagram-makeup-trend.

38 why mindful eating is so much better: Sandra Aamodt, *Why Diets Make Us Fat* (New York: Current, 2016).

44 gauge their thoughts on aging: Audrey Fine, "Depressing Study Reveals That Women Feel 'Invisible' by Age 51," Totalbeauty.com, http://www.totalbeauty.com/content/blog/depressing-study-reveals-women-feel-invisible-age-51-14.

CHAPTER THREE: I'm Not Sorry

53 96 percent of women feel guilty: Louise Eccles, "The Guilty-All-the-Time Generation: How 96 Percent of Women Feel Ashamed at Least Once a Day," *Daily Mail*, December 28, 2010, http://www.dailymail.co.uk/femail/article-1342075/The-guilty-time-generation-How-96-women-feel-ashamed-day.html.

68 a much lower threshold for what constitutes: Karina Schumann and Michael Ross, "Why Women Apologize More than Men: Gender Differences in Thresholds for Perceiving Offensive Behavior," *Psychological Science*, September 10, 2010, https://web.stanford.edu/~omidf/KarinaSchumann/KarinaSchumann_Home/Publications_files/Schumann.PsychScience.2010.pdf.

CHAPTER FOUR: Vulnerability Is a Superpower

82 "Here's the thing about being perfect": Angela Natividad, "Ad of the Day: Who Needs Perfect? Ronda Rousey Doesn't in This Intense Reebok Ad," *Adweek*, July 14, 2016, http://www.adweek.com/brand-marketing/ad-day-who-needs-perfect-ronda-rousey-doesnt-intense-reebok-ad-172506.

CHAPTER FIVE: Self-Love, Self-Sabotage, and Feeling Like a Fraud

103 "You can spend your whole life imagining": "Jim Carrey Commencement Speech: Full Video and Transcript," Maharishi University of Management,

http://www.mum.edu/whats-happening/graduation-2014/full-jim-carrey
-address-video-and-transcript, accessed March 29, 2018.

105 account for 40 to 50 percent of our happiness: L. Suval, "Happiness
and Choices," Psych Central, 2012, https://psychcentral.com/blog/happiness
-and-choices.

107 Despite external evidence: Pauline Rose Clance and Suzanne A. Imes,
"The Imposter Phenomenon in High Achieving Women: Dynamics and
Therapeutic Intervention," *Psychotherapy: Theory, Research and Practice* 15,
no. 3 (1978).

109 70 percent of people experience imposter: Breena Kerr, "Why 70%
of Millennials Have Impostor Syndrome," *The Hustle*, November 20, 2015,
http://thehustle.co/why-70-percent-of-millennials-have-impostor-syndrome.

CHAPTER SIX: Audacious Auditing

134 the role of language in self-talk: Ethan Kross, "Self-Talk as a Regula-
tory Mechanism: How You Do It Matters," *Journal of Personality and Social
Psychology* 106, no. 2 (2014).

137 every habit starts with a three-part process: Charles Duhigg, *The
Power of Habit: Why We Do What We Do in Life and Business* (New York:
Random House, 2012).

CHAPTER SEVEN: Success Is a State of Being

149 a survey done by *Glamour* magazine: Genevieve Field, "What Success Looks Like, According to *Glamour* Readers," *Glamour*, May 5, 2015,
https://www.glamour.com/story/glamour-survey-what-success-means-to-you.

161 people strive to reach $75,000: Belinda Luscombe, "Do We Need
$75,000 a Year to Be Happy?" *Time*, September 6, 2010.

167 "If you aren't willing to fight for what": Madonna, "Madonna's Back,"
Harper's Bazaar, October 4, 2013, http://www.harpersbazaar.com/celebrity
/latest/news/a1095/madonna-interview 1113.

168 Arianna has said, "You can recognize": Poppy Harlow, "Arianna Huffington Tells Women: Less Stress, More Living," CNN.com, March 8, 2013,

http://www.cnn.com/2013/03/07/business/arianna-huffington-leading
-women/index.html.

184 "Intuition is a very powerful thing": Walter Isaacson, "The Genius of Jobs," *New York Times*, October 29, 2011, http://www.nytimes.com/2011 /10/30/opinion/sunday/steve-jobss-genius.html.

184 "Learning to trust your instincts": "What Oprah Knows for Sure About Trusting Her Intuition," *O: The Oprah Magazine*, August 2011, http://www .oprah.com/spirit/oprah-on-trusting-her-intuition-oprahs-advice-on-trusting -your-gut.

187 the Association of Psychological Science reported: Lizette Borreli, "Why Using Pen and Paper, Not Laptops, Boosts Memory: Writing Notes Helps Recall Concepts, Ability to Understand," *Medical Daily*, February 6, 2014, http://www.medicaldaily.com/why-using-pen-and-paper-not-laptops -boosts-memory-writing-notes-helps-recall-concepts-ability-268770.

Don't miss Cara's field guide for the female entrepreneur, GIRL CODE.

CaraAlwill.com

Penguin Random House